# LOSE THE GUM

A Survival Guide for Women on Wall Street

## TAMARA LASHCHYK

**BALBOA.**
PRESS
A DIVISION OF HAY HOUSE

Balboa Press books may be ordered through booksellers or by contacting:

Balboa Press
A Division of Hay House
1663 Liberty Drive
Bloomington, IN 47403
www.balboapress.com
1 (877) 407-4847

Because of the dynamic nature of the Internet, any web addresses or links contained in this book may have changed since publication and may no longer be valid. The views expressed in this work are solely those of the author and do not necessarily reflect the views of the publisher, and the publisher hereby disclaims any responsibility for them.

The author of this book does not dispense medical advice or prescribe the use of any technique as a form of treatment for physical, emotional, or medical problems without the advice of a physician, either directly or indirectly. The intent of the author is only to offer information of a general nature to help you in your quest for emotional and spiritual well-being. In the event you use any of the information in this book for yourself, which is your constitutional right, the author and the publisher assume no responsibility for your actions.

Any people depicted in stock imagery provided by Thinkstock are models, and such images are being used for illustrative purposes only. Certain stock imagery © Thinkstock.

Print information available on the last page.

ISBN: 978-1-5043-7437-8 (sc)
ISBN: 978-1-5043-7438-5 (e)

Library of Congress Control Number: 2017901990

Balboa Press rev. date: 02/27/2017

And to all the little girls watching right now, never doubt
that you are valuable and powerful and deserving
of every chance and opportunity in the world
to pursue and achieve your own dreams.

—Hillary Rodham Clinton
November 9, 2016

# CONTENTS

# INTRODUCTION

> "The majority of modern women have been cut off from the flow of their feminine energy and refuse its healing and grace. Without the feminine strengths of compassion, abundance, and kindness ruling our hearts, we neglect and abuse ourselves. Like nomads wandering in a desert of competition, dissatisfaction, and lack, we attempt to find solace in the masculine traits of force, aggressiveness, and dominance."
>
> —Unknown

**THROUGHOUT MY CAREER ON** Wall Street, I've worked with many brilliant and talented women whom I respected for their ability to burgeon in this high-powered, yet challenging profession. But I have also watched as so many women have fumbled about trying to find their footing in Wall Street's masculine world. Women have been taught that the embodiment of certain female behaviors puts us at a disadvantage against our male counterparts, and so we don't embrace our feminine qualities in the workplace. Instead, we either stifle these qualities or we overcompensate by taking on masculine traits. But in either case, these actions aren't inherently natural to us and prevent us from harnessing the full potential of our feminine power. This limits our capabilities and can directly translate into fewer pay increases, promotions, and opportunities for mobility. Essentially, we are standing in our own way.

While our behaviors shut us out of opportunities, the lack of awareness also plays a role, as we sabotage ourselves and destroy our chances for what could have been a vibrant career. Every woman contributes to the overall female business statistics and every woman who has left the workplace is part of the reason why these statistics haven't improved in a meaningful way in more than a generation. A recent study[1] by McKinsey and LeanIn.org shows that, at the current rate of change, it will take women 100 years to reach parity in the C-suite. All research supports a business case for gender diversity, yet every workplace study ever conducted on gender equality shows that women are at a disadvantage. This is not an excuse, but a fact that is changing at a painfully slow rate.

I've witnessed these statistics in the making first hand as I've watched many talented women walk out the door and opt-out of this industry altogether. Because diverse organizations foster greater innovation, creativity, and bottom line results, the

---

[1]  In 2015 McKinsey & Company and LeanIn.org conducted a survey of 30,000 workers at 118 North American companies. The year over year improvement in the statistics was used to calculate the rate at which women will reach parity.

financial services industry with its limited female perspective, has missed out on an immeasurable amount of contributions. And while some women leave this industry because of personal life choices, many women leave out of frustration and hopelessness (though they may still hide behind the label of "life choices"). I was raised to believe that opportunity should be available to anyone who wants it and leaving the workforce because you feel that you have no options is, to me, entirely unacceptable.

As I rose through the ranks in Wall Street, I saw more opportunities afforded to men than to women. Even though I was often allowed into the boys club, I still felt that men had an unfair advantage because of their gender. And while my father had always preached that life wasn't necessarily fair, I wanted to have the same opportunities that were available to men, regardless. I was among the few privileged women to be included in many of the inner circles (aka the boy's clubs), but I refused to let my willful blindness turn into plausible deniability. So, I did what I could to promote inclusion. I challenged management by drawing their attention to examples of inequities in order to force a more balanced ratio. My objective was to create an environment where women felt supported, so I also spent countless hours mentoring and coaching young women. But at the end of the day, I still watched helplessly as too many women would exit this industry.

After twenty something years in this business, I realized that all women face the same challenges because we are all trying to navigate a system of protocols that never took us into consideration in the first place. I wrote *Lose the Gum* to raise awareness of these protocols and to offer some guidance on how to steer through them. In a hierarchical environment, the "rules" or established protocols aren't always clear, and missteps along the corporate path can be damaging to your career. I know that the playing field isn't level, but in writing this book, I hope to tilt the scales a little closer to the middle and lay the groundwork for other women to balance them completely.

This book is meant to be a practical guide to outline the unwritten rules of Wall Street's corporate culture and offer some ideas on how to manage perceptions within these protocols. This is merely a guideline and isn't meant to be a panacea that guarantees success, nor does it inoculate against failure. I also offer no delusions about being your authentic self or the belief that if you are true to yourself, corporate culture will embrace you, *because, from my experience, it probably will not*. It may even chew you up and spit you out. But that doesn't mean that you should sell out either because you should never change your core values for anyone or anything. It simply means that you need to understand the consequences of your actions in order to make a conscious decision about which core values and which character traits you allow yourself to reveal in order to create your professional identity. It is important to be able to recognize this distinction so you can preserve who you are as a person. Always keep in mind that although your career is important, it's not who you are; it's only what you do. As such, you should always protect your core beliefs and treasure your sense of self. Under no circumstance, should you ever give away any piece of your soul.

# MY ROAD TO THE STREET

**FOR AS LONG AS** I can remember, I've wanted to work on Wall Street. I graduated college in the early nineties while the financial services industry was still recovering from the hangover of the housing bubble burst. The economy was in a recession and unemployment hovered at around seven percent. As a new college grad, unable to find a job, I was frustrated and disillusioned by a system that had promised so much and yet offered so little. I felt like the excess that was reaped by the previous generations left little for the next, and all I wanted was my fair share. Despite the challenging job market, I was resolute about working on Wall Street and once I had embraced that commitment, I chased after it with unwavering fervor.

I was first introduced to the world of investment banking through my university's cooperative education program. This program gave me the opportunity to work on Wall Street during each of my college years. For my first co-op, I landed a job at the prestigious international law firm of Davis Polk & Wardwell. There, I worked around the clock assisting with M&A deals, which, as an intern, mostly meant making copies, faxing, and of course picking up food orders. Nevertheless, I got to work in the cone of secrecy on private side deals that, once announced, would grace the pages of the Wall Street Journal. *How cool was that?*

Davis Polk's clients were various bulge bracket investment banks. While working on live deals, I spent countless hours with some of the "iBanking" analysts. We worked well into the night and often times on weekends. During those grueling hours, I evaluated each firm based on how their employees treated me, as well as how they treated one another. Some of the employees were arrogant and conceited, some were aggressive and brash and some were just plain assholes. But ONE firm in particular stood out and made a positive impression on me. That firm was JP Morgan. JP Morgan was white-shoed and blue-blooded, and its employees were intelligent, impeccably dressed, and always well mannered. So I set my sights on getting a job at JP Morgan, despite having no real pedigree myself.

In order to achieve this goal, I systematically sent my resume to JP Morgan's Personnel Department every week, and every week I would systematically receive a rejection letter. At some point, my friends and family even tried to persuade me to give up on what they said was a pipe dream, but that only fueled my determination even more.

Time continued to progress and with each passing day without a paycheck, my bills and college loans began to accumulate. My financial situation grew dire. Out of desperation, I was forced to put my aspirations of working at JP Morgan on hold and take any job that I could find. So I accepted a position at the local Acme, where I was hired to bag groceries. To me, this was a huge blow. I was so close to grabbing the brass ring, but now it seemed further away than ever. I sank to my lowest depths, mainly because I felt that menial labor was beneath me. But as it turned out, it offered me one of the most valuable life lessons I would ever learn. The experience humbled me and kept me grounded, even as I advanced my own financial and social status. Even now when my environment tends to get uppity, it brings me back down to earth and serves as a reminder to just keep it real.

When I first met my fellow Acme employees, I thought our backgrounds and goals were dissimilar. But upon getting to know them, I discovered that we weren't so different after all. I came to learn that while some worked at Acme because it was a suitable life choice for their families, there were some who, just like me, were taken off course due to life's circumstances; but we were all bound by the same common thread and I wasn't better than anyone else. I learned that there is nothing demeaning about honest work for honest pay; **this is** a lesson that I still embrace today.

No matter who you are, rich or poor, everyone needs to eat and, therefore, everyone shops for groceries. I met people from all walks of life including war veterans, immigrants, people with disabilities, the rich and poor, politicians, local celebrities, and sports stars such as local news anchor, Lisa Thomas Laury and basketball legend, Charles Barkley. Every person had his or her own unique and compelling story, which I found to be infinitely interesting. And because the tasks of the job weren't providing me with intellectual stimulation, I satiated my thirst for curiosity by learning about people.

One of the more remarkable individuals I met was Ms. Vivian. She was a feisty elderly woman who lost her vision due to macular degeneration. She had unbelievable resolve and was adamant about taking care of herself by shopping for her own groceries. Each week, Ms. Vivian took a bus from Center City to the Acme. When she arrived, she would always ask for me, not necessarily by name, but she would refer to me as "that charming young lady," a remark that pleased me because I knew it would have made my mother proud. I would then patiently escort her around and lend her my vision so she could choose the items she wanted. My time with Ms. Vivian was fulfilling and although she needed my help, I always looked forward to her visits on Wednesdays because, in many ways, I needed her too.

I also recall a Korean War Veteran named Barry. He once asked me to assemble a fan that he had just purchased because he had one wooden hand and knew that he would struggle. Amidst the sweltering heat and humidity of the Philadelphia summer, I obliged him and with immense gratitude, he tipped me $20. Initially, I refused the money because he seemed somewhat impoverished, always wearing the same stained undershirt and smelling like tuna fish. But when he offered again, my own dire straits pushed aside greater decency and I took the money. At the time, I was only making about $6 an hour, but I still shouldn't have taken it. It was one of those moments that I wished I had done differently, but not significant enough to harbor regret. Working at Acme has given me countless stories like these. I can remember everyone because each of them had a profound impact on me. The entire experience helped shape who I am, not only in my personality but who I am at my core.

Although there was something gratifying about my job at Acme, it didn't squelch my ambitions of working at JP Morgan – *not for a second*. The very first thing I did when I got home every day was check my answering machine. I anxiously hoped that someone from JP Morgan had called - *but they didn't, at least not that day.* My boyfriend's mother, who had an intuitive intelligence, assured me that the offer would come.

"But when?" I would ask with hopelessness in my eyes and a frown on my forehead, as if she knew the answer to my divine question. In a sense, though, she did. She told me that the offer would come when I was ready and when I had learned all that I was supposed to learn from this experience. This was another valuable lesson that I would come to accept, but not until later in life. I was not yet ready to understand its deeper spiritual context at the time.

So, I went to work and became a diligent student of life's lessons in hopes that it would speed up the arrival of my offer. In the meantime, I put my best foot forward and did the finest job that I could. If I was bagging groceries, my goal was to make sure all the items were neatly parceled by the time the last one came down the conveyor. If I was asked to tidy the parking lot, I collapsed all the carts to form perfectly straight rows and freed the ground of every last piece of litter. I rather enjoyed the tasks that allowed me to be outside and was glad to have a temporary reprieve from the monotony of bagging groceries. Just like prisoners who revel in the sunshine as they pick up trash on the side of the highway, being outdoors gave a momentary sense of freedom.

I kept my spirits high and all my hard work was eventually noticed when I caught the attention of Acme's management. They even offered me an opportunity for advancement through the Management Training Program. I, however, had a different career path in mind for myself, so I declined the offer. The offer from JP Morgan did eventually come but it wasn't an easy path or a straight road. When I finally did quit the job at Acme, I tried to return my smock to the store manager, but in a playful attempt at being smug, he told me to keep it, just in case I needed to come back. My reaction was cavalier, although my nervous laugh confirmed that I knew it was true. With the economy in its current state, no job was guaranteed. And that little bit of insecurity is what has always kept me motivated while rejecting complacency. It is this constant hustle that has kept me employed, even through the worst economic cycles.

I used to think that my career began with my job at JP Morgan, but I later came to realize that all the steps that I took along the way played a critical role in my career. Every experience shapes who we are and each life event, whether we like it or not, becomes the impetus that drives our motivations and sets our intentions. These events can inspire us and impact the decisions that we make, both consciously and subconsciously.

When I started at JP Morgan, I was incredibly grateful for the job and never once took it for granted. I was also enamored by the idea of Wall Street and all the cache that came with it. The work was dynamic and interesting, the pace was fast and energetic, the industry was lucrative and the people were some of the smartest on the planet. Each role brought challenges that inspired me intellectually and fostered my ambition. And because I was so infatuated with Wall Street and worked so hard to get there, in the beginning, I was willfully blind to some of its less positive traits. Even thinking one negative thought about the industry that I admired so deeply, in my mind, would have been a sacrilege. So I lived in denial and struggled to navigate a system that was highly political, male-dominated, and sexist.

In the early years of my career, I didn't quite know how to steer clear of obstacles and pitfalls. I frequently made mistakes that at times impacted the trajectory of my career. I often wished that someone would have given me honest advice and told me straight up how things really were. Instead, I received guidance in the form of politically motivated corporate rhetoric. For a while, I subscribed to this and even towed the party line, but at some point, I grew tired of playing along. Although I loved every job that I had and approached each one with unbridled passion, I was still left feeling somewhat unfulfilled. A corporation will never care for you to the extent that you care for it or your job, so I came to realize that I was never going to get the emotional gratification that I was seeking. At this point, I knew that I was going to have to change my approach. But first, I was going to have to take back my soul, which I felt I had given away far too easily.

This shift in attitude was transformational because I stopped operating from a place that was so deeply tied to my own vulnerability. I began to see each situation with greater objectivity and clarity. I started to understand how motives drive decisions and I was able to recognize intentions. I even began to understand my own motives and what drove my own behaviors. But more importantly, I began to understand the qualities that were valued by the company so I could choose to behave in a way that aligned with these corporate values. I learned that I could control the perceptions that others formed about me by choosing my actions carefully and strategically. Once I understood all of this, operating within the context of this environment became much easier. However, as I watched and observed, I saw countless women still struggling in this arena.

# LOSE THE GUM

**A FEW YEARS IN** and I was on my way to building a successful career. I was still very much infatuated by the industry, so I turned a blind eye to some of its less appealing qualities, sexism among them. In the beginning, I hadn't really noticed because I grew up in a household filled with boys and felt right at home in Wall Street's male-dominated setting. I was even granted access to many of the boy's clubs while my personality lent itself well to the rough and tumble habitat of the trading floor. My career was advancing, so I never really thought that my opportunities were limited based on my gender. But once I discovered that my compensation was less than that of my male counterparts, even when I was ranked higher in terms of performance, that's when I started paying attention. At the end of the day, I realized that I wasn't any different than any other woman and that we all faced the same challenges and struggles. No matter how accepted I was with the guys, I was still subjected to sexism and discrimination. And let me tell you, it sucked.

Discrimination appears in different forms, but in a corporate environment, one of the most challenging forms to combat is subtle bias. Unlike blatant discrimination, which can be addressed with corrective measures, subtle bias is based on attitude, which makes it difficult to prove and even harder to fix. Subtle bias is rooted in an unconscious belief that you may not even realize you have and it rears its ugly head in the way you behave. In the case of gender bias, there is an underlying belief that men are superior to women. It is this very belief that puts women at a disadvantage right from the outset because it creates an unfair difference in how women are treated. It also develops a perception that unless disproven, can very quickly become a reality. It is, therefore, important for women in business to pay close attention to their actions and try to eliminate the behaviors that defend gender bias.

When it comes to behaviors that form negative impressions, chewing gum obviously isn't going to eliminate gender bias, nor will it make or break your career. However, chewing gum in any milieu is an unappealing habit. When it comes to creating a professional image, chewing gum breaches a woman's overall appearance and cheapens her look. I chose the title "Lose the Gum" not because I have issues with gum chewers, but as a metaphor to represent the inflection point when a girl makes a conscious decision to take action and become a professional woman.

In one of my first supervisory positions, I managed a middle-office team in Emerging Markets. The business was growing rapidly and I needed to hire in order to keep up with the pace of growth. But I also had to be selective and ensure that I hired someone who could handle the pressures of the job. High trading volumes, grueling hours, and market volatility created intensity, while mistakes in our business have monetary consequences that could run in the millions. That alone is a lot of stress to bear; add a screaming trader to the mix and you have a pressure cooker.

It really does take a certain type of person who can work in Wall Street's taxing environment and excel under the pressure of its rigor. And that was the type of person I was looking for: someone who would thrive in a high-stress domain.

I gathered about one and a half dozen resumes from both internal and external candidates and I carefully reviewed each one. Careless mistakes and sloppiness were the first standards for elimination, so any resume with typos was immediately tossed out. Any candidate that expressed interest in the job but then dragged their feet in sending me their resume was also eliminated. Candidates that didn't call me back within 24 hours were also crossed off the list. Just by this process alone, I was able to eliminate about 25% of the candidates right from the get go. Those who were assertive and followed up with phone calls or stopped by my office were moved to the top of the list; I was looking for hunger.

In reviewing the resumes, I took into account grade point averages based on major and school. I also considered any unique qualifications or achievements that demonstrated the attributes needed to succeed. The resume review brought the list of contenders down another 25%. During the interview process, two candidates were eliminated before they even answered one question. One was late for the interview with no excuse or apology. The other was eliminated because he looked like he had just rolled out of bed, bleary-eyed and disheveled, and wearing a suit that he looked like he had slept in.

In the end, I narrowed the field down to two candidates. The top contender was pretty much a shoe-in for the job because along with a strong resume, she was an internal referral from a colleague of mine. For the interview, she came in dressed professionally in the standard corporate uniform of the navy blue suit. But as she approached me to shake my hand, I noticed that she was chewing gum. As she spoke, that big wad of gum juggled from side to side in her mouth. I found it to be very distracting. I also couldn't help but wonder why she might have thought it was a good idea to chew gum during an interview. I then questioned her judgment, which led to an entire slew of inferences. In the end, I couldn't get past it, so I ended up not hiring her. When I reflected on the situation, I thought how unfortunate it was for her to lose out on an opportunity over something so trivial. I pondered my decision and wondered whether I had made the right call or had I been too quick to judge? But I also reminded myself of how competitive this industry is and that every factor is fair game when it comes to differentiating yourself from others.

It doesn't take much to form an impression. According to Malcolm Gladwell, in his book *Blink,* most people practice *thin-slicing*[2]. We process information quickly and automatically and make decisions and assessments from the strengths of our adaptive unconscious. In other words, we make snap judgments. We are uncomfortable with ambiguity, so we use whatever slivers of information are available to us and then fill in the gaps with assumptions.

---

[2]    *Thin-slicing-the ability to make decisions or judgments based on a narrow piece of information*

Later that year, I participated in the cross-divisional performance review committee wherein a select number of managers were asked to review all associates across every division in order to ensure consistency. It was there that I had the opportunity to hear feedback on the gum-chewing associate. Through this process, I found out that while the quality of her work product was solid, she had a very difficult personality. She was emotionally volatile and would frequently throw temper tantrums that ended in tears. She required constant re-assurance to prevent meltdowns and to keep her from unraveling under the pressure of the job. When I heard this feedback, I was so relieved that I hadn't hired her and felt like I had dodged a bullet.

I came to understand that although it was the gum that caught my conscious attention, it was my instincts that picked up on something much more subtle, that I didn't consciously even realize. And that is how the world works and people form judgments based on all sorts of things. Some of these reasons are conscious, but most often they are not. And whether we like it or not, we are all predisposed to some type of judgement.

Most people underestimate the importance of professionalism, but it truly is required for success. Professionalism alone won't carry you to success, but lacking it could be the sole reason for failure. The good news is that professionalism is entirely within your control. It is a learned behavior, practiced over time that eventually becomes part of your muscle memory. As such, it is best to develop good habits early on in your career, so they become second nature to you. Your professionalism and ALL your behaviors create your image, your reputation, and your brand. In business, your reputation is a form of currency. A stellar reputation could open doors for you, while a bad or tainted reputation could shut you out. And remember: your reputation almost always precedes you.

I have stressed the importance of this to many women that I've mentored, as I try to help women gain every advantage possible on a playing field dominated by men. But often times, I have felt that women stand in their own way and make it harder for themselves to grasp the opportunities that are there for the taking. It doesn't take a lot of effort to form a positive impression. But if you fail to recognize the importance of professionalism to success, you may end up unconsciously choosing inappropriate behaviors. Many times creating a positive impression only requires a slight shift in actions, but that shift can only occur if there is awareness.

# BRAND BUILDING

**I FELT LIKE THE** day that JP Morgan merged with the Chase was the day that my beloved firm had died. A quagmire of retail bank mergers from the Chase enterprise now perverted the once pristine investment bank that was the House of Morgan. Dissatisfied by the new combined firm, I considered the possibility of leaving the only firm at which I had ever wanted to work.

The last job I had at JP Morgan was in Human Resources. As someone who came up through the ranks of the business, I lacked the softer touch that was expected from an HR professional. I was assertive and plowed forward. Consequently, I became known as the "bulldozer." But I was effective in getting the job done, so my style was supported and encouraged. But after the acquisition of JP Morgan, the environment became deeply rooted in the existing Chase culture, and my style was perceived to be too aggressive.

Early on, I was competing with "the boys," so I developed a manner that was equally as aggressive as their testosterone driven behaviors. I also didn't know that personal style had any impact on my career whatsoever. I always believed that the end result was the only important measure of performance. I approached every project with an intensity that focused only on achieving results and paid no mind to the undercurrent of corporate politics. But as it turned out, the "how" was equally as, if not more important than, the "what." As a result, I made plenty of mistakes. At times, I felt like breaking protocol was even more damaging to my career than if I had outright broken some of the rules. It took me years to realize this, and by the time I finally got it, I had done so much harm to my career that I almost didn't recover.

I finally did decide to leave JP Morgan and joined Merrill Lynch. Merrill was going through a growth spurt and the firm was building up its investment bank. The stock price was soaring. One of my mentors had just been hired there, and she asked me to come and work for her and raved about the firm and its culture. While interviewing, I felt a wave of energy and enthusiasm from the firm's employees. It felt like everyone who worked there really wanted to be there, and that made me want to be there too. There was a sense of company pride and I was excited to be a part of it all. I once again found a firm where I thought I could fit in and climb to the next level of my career. I felt like I had found my new home.

Upon leaving JP Morgan, I received one of the most valuable pieces of advice of my career. It was from our Diversity Executive and she tried to pose it in the form of a thought-provoking question. But as you can't make a horse drink, I missed her point. She had asked me what I wanted my new brand to be when I joined my new company. She said that I would have the opportunity to completely re-brand myself in my new job and that I should think carefully about how perceptions were formed. I'll never forget this conversation, but I shrugged off her advice at the time because I had no idea what she was even talking about.

When I arrived at Merrill Lynch, I was extremely focused on delivering results. During my first two months, I met with the top twenty-five most senior leaders in Global Markets. I was confident as an expert in my field and was equally confident having worked at one of the best firms on Wall Street. I brought premium experience and cutting-edge knowledge to Merrill and used every opportunity to explain how things were done at JP Morgan. My new Merrill colleagues didn't really appreciate that and much of what I had to say went over like a lead balloon.

But I worked very hard and forged forward. After six months at Merrill, I launched two programs with enormous levels of success. The first was a continuing education program, which was attended by close to 5,000 sales & trading professionals. If you know how traders are, you would understand what an enormous feat it was to have that type of turnout for a program that wasn't compulsory. The other program was around innovation and it made such a tremendous impact that the CEO mandated that every business across the firm implement some version of the program. I was knocking the cover off the ball, yet it seemed that my career was dangling by a string. In order to get things done, I found myself bulldozing through the bureaucracy and frequently going around people, instead of working through the team structure. I broke glass every step of the way and pissed people off at every corner. There was always a lot of noise surrounding me and my methods. I delivered outstanding results, but my manner nearly cost me my career.

At the end of the year, when I sat down with my boss to

receive my performance review, on a five-point scale (five being the best), I was rated a three. I was devastated. I had poured my heart and soul into this job and had yielded tremendous results, only to receive more criticism than accolades. It wasn't enough just to produce a great work product; I was also expected to deliver these results in a way that adhered to the corporate culture.

My saving grace was that my internal clients thought that I did an outstanding job, and they ultimately came to my defense. They made an arrangement with HR Management to hire me a coach, who would teach me how to play nice in the sandbox. I agreed to work with the coach, but I thought it was all complete and total bullshit. Then one day, I decided to tell my coach exactly that. She reacted by snapping back and said point-blank, "If you don't change your style, they are going to fire you." For some reason, this caught my attention. I suppose I had what they call a coming to Jesus moment because I finally saw the light.

I asked my coach to help me, and she agreed. She taught me all about brand-building and its importance in business, particularly in corporate environments. She also taught me how to develop a style that was consistent with the brand that I was trying to create. She helped me develop a style that worked well with Merrill's relational culture and helped me to rebrand myself altogether.

It wasn't going to be easy, though, because I had achieved great success throughout my career and had established my behavior patterns. Now, I was going to have to break habits and learn new behaviors. I was essentially going to have to re-create my professional identity from the ground up. Furthermore, I wasn't entirely convinced that a milder version of myself would be the best fit for Wall Street. I was concerned that I would lose my edge and, subsequently, my ability to be effective in my job. I had purposefully created a tough work persona in order to protect myself from the fierce environment. Now, I was going to have to show parts of my personality that I didn't necessarily want to reveal at work. And that scared me. But what I was currently doing wasn't working, and despite the challenges I was facing, I really did enjoy my job at Merrill and I wanted to continue to work there. But then I remembered my former mentor who was the soft-spoken head of HR. She had a mind like a steel trap and was powerful as all hell. Even though she never raised her voice, the power of her strength was felt whenever she walked in a room. That was the style I wanted to create for myself, so I kept a mental picture of her actions in my mind and tried to emulate her behaviors as much as possible. I also knew this wasn't going to be THAT difficult because I already had a softer side that I just kept hidden. I even had a side that was laid back and chill; for heaven's sake, I practiced meditation long before it was even a popular trend. So I drew from within and developed a style that was more palatable to my co-workers.

In the beginning, I felt vulnerable, like a house cat that was being de-clawed and sent into the wild. But with practice, my new behaviors took hold and became second nature. The response was very positive and I was able to develop better, more trusting relationships with my colleagues. I continued to refine my brand throughout the years by paying attention to the impression I was leaving on people. I kept an idea of the image that I wanted to portray at the forefront of my mind and chose behaviors that would cause that impression to take hold.

I took full accountability for my behaviors and didn't shrug off my bad habits as if they were a personality dysfunction that had no cure. I recognized that we are in control of our actions and therefore we are each responsible for our behaviors.

I finally understood how important a personal brand is to your career. Building a brand to succeed in the corporate world may include making a conscious decision about which character traits you allow yourself to reveal. But it's important to recognize the difference between carefully choosing to reveal certain aspects of your already existing personality and totally compromising your core values by pretending to be something that you're not. And although you may be able to fool some people, most of the people around you will sense your lack of sincerity and they won't trust you. So in the end being disingenuous or phony will not serve you well. And you can trust me on that.

# NEVER LET 'EM SEE YA SWEAT

**WHEN I ARRIVED AT** Merrill, I had what I believed was a brilliant idea for a program on the topic of financial services innovation. The program would be launched on a global scale, across the entire Global Markets Business. It had the potential for an 8,000-person participation rate, with enormous visibility. I pitched the idea to the head of Global Markets who liked it very much but was skeptical about its challenging execution. To put his mind at ease, I decided to seek endorsement from one of his direct reports. With that in mind, I brought the idea to the co-head of Fixed Income Currencies and Commodities ("FICC"), whose rock-star status made him hugely influential within the business. He liked the idea but was totally risk averse, and the sheer scale of the program scared him. He also questioned the program's execution with its many moving parts across multiple regions. It was risky, and he didn't want to be associated with something that he thought might fail.

But I knew I was good at my job, and I had the experience needed to execute a program as complex as this one. Plus, I had thought through every last detail of the implementation and knew exactly how I was going to pull this off. Self-efficacy kept me driving forward with intense focus, and I paid no attention to the skepticism that was being raised by the other business heads. Through perseverance, passion, and conviction, I got them all to buy in.

But their doubts somehow managed to seep into my head, and I began to second-guess myself. Once I got all the required sign-offs, I went home and literally threw up. I was rattled and unnerved and was having a momentary crisis of confidence. I wrestled with doubt the whole night through and tossed and turned sleeplessly through anxiety filled dreams that ended with night terrors.

The next day, I went to work and told the co-head of FICC about my stress and anxiety, at which time I think HE went home and threw up. He had just agreed to champion a program with a leader who seemed unsure of herself and who doubted the project's success. He saw visions of the program failing on an enormous scale and, with it, his popularity going down in flames. I could see the color draining from his face. I realized right then and there that sharing my stress with him was a bad decision. It was at that very moment that I learned that you should never let 'em see ya sweat.

Confidence is an essential characteristic, especially when you're in a position of leadership. No one wants to turn to the captain of a sinking ship only to find him curled up in a fetal ball of panic. And when the end is imminent, most people prefer a fearless leader who will bravely lead them, even if it's through a delusional sense of hope and optimism. People feel more comfortable working with those who are confident in their abilities than with people who are unsure of themselves. In business, men and women alike respect women who have confidence. Confidence puts people at ease and provides them with a sense of security and trust. No one wants to do business with someone who doubts herself or seems afraid. This is especially true in finance where the stakes are high and money is at risk. In reality, everyone is pretty much afraid, maybe not all the time, but certainly some of the time. Feeling afraid is normal, but showing fear can be the kiss of death.

So where does confidence come from? Well, to understand confidence and other similar qualities, we will have to poke around the human psyche and speak in psychobabble. A discussion that touches upon the human psyche is relevant because, while most career books offer practical advice, they tend to ignore the realm of the human condition. Yet, what often stands between us and success is not just circumstances, but rather what lies within our psyche. Our emotions, our fears, and our insecurities stand in our way, and they are all in our head. Actually, they *are* our head.

> The toughest opponent of all is the one inside your head
>
> —Joe Henderson

The psyche of a woman is often her greatest foe. Women tend to overthink and overanalyze, which can become paralyzing. Unlike other aspects of life where introspection is required for self-growth, in business too much introspection can be detrimental. It can intensify fears and create limiting self-images that lead to feelings of doubt and behaviors of self-sabotage. Before you know it, you've concocted a toxic cocktail of defeat.

Confidence, self-efficacy, and self-esteem are three very important qualities that are often mistakenly believed to be the same thing. But they are not. They are distinctly different. We gain a sense of self-efficacy when we see ourselves mastering skills and achieving goals that matter, while self-esteem is our own assessment of our worth. Together these qualities contribute to self-confidence.

To understand these qualities, we need to take a look back to when they were formed, which any good shrink will tell you was during childhood. We were all born with purity of thought and knowledge of our own greatness. But then the world took its toll and perversely re-programmed our patterns of thinking to make us all think less of ourselves. Our minds became cluttered with negative ideas and limiting self-images, which morphed into what we call self-esteem.

For me, my self-esteem came from my mother, who herself struggled with her own issues of low self-worth. She grew up in the background of two talented sisters and felt that she had little to offer the world. She married my father, who was a smart man and whom she admired for his intelligence. I was my father's daughter and had his intellect, so my mother looked up to me as well. Growing up, I always sensed her admiration of me as she hung on my every word. *It made me feel smart and very special.* And when the world overwhelmed me and became almost too heavy to bear, my mother was right beside me whispering in my ear, "You can do it." Those were powerful words to constantly hear from a parent. And after an entire childhood filled with these types of whispers, I grew up believing I could do it. *Anyone would, as long as the other parent wasn't saying, "Shut up, stupid."*

Our formative years lay the groundwork for the development of self-esteem. Once it is formed, it is hard to change because it is deeply rooted in our psyche. Low self-esteem and feelings of inadequacy aren't necessarily remedied by success or any other external factors because they are driven by fear and insecurity, not logical reasoning. But everyone has feelings of doubt and flashes of low self-worth; this is the case with both men and women. My friend owns and operates a two and a half-million-dollar company, and once in a while, he'll say to me, "It's not bad for a loser." As you look up the success chain, you will find more of the same. I once saw an interview with fashion icon Diane Von Furstenberg and she said that you never feel the success, and you always think that things are going wrong. She said, "So many mornings I wake up, and I feel like a loser, and I ask other people who are successful, 'Do you ever feel like a loser?' and they say, 'Yeah.'" And two of the smartest and most successful colleagues that I've ever known told me that they frequently wake up in the middle of the night to the same recurring dream that the world has discovered that they are a fraud. I'm not sure these feelings ever go away. Even the most confident people have flashes of doubts and panic sometimes.

Because confidence and self-esteem are closely entwined, having low self-esteem will affect your sense of confidence. But unlike self-esteem, which comes from within, confidence is about behavior and has more to do with external factors. Confidence can be strong, but it can also be very fragile. Confidence needs to be frequently replenished because it is not constant. Confidence fluctuates based on our ratio of successes to failures.

While self-esteem and self-efficacy are about how you feel, confidence is about how you act. This is important because, as we've discussed in previous chapters, how you act is within your control. Therefore, it is entirely possible to act confidently, even if you don't feel confident. So yes, you can actually fake confidence. I wouldn't, however, suggest doing it all the time because you cannot consistently perform in a way that is inconsistent with how you see yourself. But you can fake confidence just enough to get you through certain situations as long as you never let 'em see ya sweat.

# IMAGE IS EVERYTHING

**AFTER GETTING SENIOR MANAGEMENT'S** buy-in for the Innovation Program, I began to plan its launch. I was also able to convince the co-head of FICC to become my champion, despite his initial concerns. As I worked through the details and overcame my crisis of confidence, I began to believe the program had the potential to be a tremendous success, and I was excited by the prospects. To launch the program, I scheduled a kick-off meeting to gather all the key stakeholders and walk them through the idea and the logistics of the execution.

On the morning of the kick-off, I woke up with a touch of the flu. I'd had a terrible night's sleep through fever and sweat, but sick or not, I was going to be at that meeting. I refused to miss the chance to present on a program that I was so passionate about. I knew that my enthusiasm would carry me through, so I mustered up my strength and got dressed for success. And that day, "dressing for success" came in the form of my favorite outfit of the season: a black knit Missoni dress. It was very professional and demure.

I arrived at Merrill's downtown headquarters just before 7 a.m. I got out of the taxi and walked straight past the construction workers who were building the mecca that would soon become Goldman's new headquarters. I walked into the Financial Center and passed by the long line of people queued up at Starbucks for their morning jolt of caffeine. A co-worker rode up the looooong escalator with me. I passed the security guards, and we exchanged our usual morning salutations. Then, I walked through Merrill's turnstiles and into an elevator where a handful of people already stood and proceeded to my office on the 15th floor.

I spent the next several minutes pulling my meeting notes together, preparing, and meditating. Before heading down to the meeting, I popped into the ladies room for one last glance in the mirror. What I saw in my reflection was alarming, to say the least. My beautiful black knit dress that hugged every curve of my body was completely sheer from the waist down. I had forgotten to put on the slip that went under the dress, and my black thong panties were fully visible. It looked like an outfit that Lady Gaga would wear to The Grammys.

I gasped, I gulped, and I skittishly kept turning around like a puppy chasing its tail, hoping that somehow the rest of my dress would miraculously appear. But it didn't. I closed my eyes tightly, praying I was dreaming. But I wasn't. My heart stopped, then it raced; I instantly felt overheated and nauseous. I quickly ran out of the bathroom and into my office, crisscrossing every step in order to keep my back against the wall, while my hands covered my crotch like two fig leaves. I buried myself behind my desk and frantically searched for a solution. "What to do? What to do? What to do?" I mumbled over and over again.

I called my boss' office, terrified. Half a second later, she stood in my doorway with a "Where's the fire?" look on her face. I tried to explain, but the words were muddled with breathlessness, and I was unable to articulate my predicament. She looked understandably confused. From her vantage point and with the convenient disguise of my desk, everything looked normal. I knew the only way to make her understand was to show her, so I stood up and twirled around like a ballerina. She gasped, "Oh my god! Ok, ok!" Now she got it. Then another look washed over her face. She was questioning my wardrobe selection as if I had consciously chosen this outfit. Hysteria and drama momentarily overshadowed her ability to reason, but when rational thinking returned, she realized that it was all a mistake and that something had gone terribly wrong. After the initial shock wore off, we agree that she would host the kick-off meeting, and I would stay hidden in my office. And so, off she went, literally leaving me behind.

I picked up the phone and began to call my co-worker Chong. Chong also happened to be my best friend, who I had met while working at JP Morgan and who had joined Merrill shortly after I did. His office was just across a narrow hallway from mine, but it was still early and he hadn't arrived at work yet. I tried calling his cell phone but there was no answer; I called incessantly – *like every 20 seconds or so.*

While I waited for him to call me back, I replayed the morning's events trying to figure out how and when everything went so wrong. I recalled taking the slip of the dress off its hanger and placing it on my bed. Suddenly that picture was stomped out by the image of me getting out of the taxi and that's when the horror set in. I thought about all the people I had seen that morning and, more importantly, all the people who had seen me. The reel played through my head in fast-forward: the construction workers, the people at Starbucks, the colleague who stood one step behind me on the escalator, the security guards, and the co-workers from the elevator. Oh my god, how many people had seen me? And what exactly did they see? Did anyone even notice? Everything had seemed so normal! Was it possible that no one had noticed? Are people really so oblivious? I *so* wanted to believe it, but I had a hard time convincing myself that I was really that lucky.

Suddenly, my office door swung open; it was Chong, and he looked as dazed and confused as ever. "Yo man, whaz goin' on? Why you keep callin' like crazy woman?" He said in a Chinese-Brooklyn accent. I tried to explain, but all I got was grunts of "Huh?? Wha???" and other half expressions that told me he had no clue why I was hysterically rambling on and on. So, I stood up and did the same twirl that I had done for my boss just a few minutes earlier. He stood silently for a moment. His eyes LIT UP and with a dirty grin, he said, "Do that again, please!"

The point of this story is that wardrobe malfunctions do happen. They happen in real life to real people, not just to attention-grabbing celebrities in Hollywood. This situation was probably my worst case of accidental nudity, but it certainly wasn't the only wardrobe glitch that I've ever had in the office. Split skirts, broken heels, running stockings, button pops, and more—wardrobe snafus just happen. Over the span of an entire career, I can guarantee they will happen to you as well. And when they happen to you, just keep calm and carry on. You may also want to keep an emergency kit in your desk that includes the following: a needle and thread, extra buttons, safety pins, safety pins, safety pins (I can't tell you how many times a safety pin has saved my ass), a Tide Stain Removing Pen, a lint brush (although in a pinch you could use scotch tape), and clear nail polish.

My story ended with minimal drama, as I was able to get in touch with my Aunt Vera, who went to my apartment and brought me the bottom half of my dress. I stayed in my office until she arrived in order to prevent further damage. I considered myself lucky that I went to the ladies room before that meeting because if I hadn't, this story would have had an entirely different ending. I shudder to think of it.

Wardrobe malfunctions are accidental, and as such, they are forgivable. But what is *not forgivable is* the conscious decision to display a lack of judgment when dressing professionally. Poor fashion choices could result in being passed over for a job or a promotion, so they are far worse than the unintentional glitch.

In business, it is important to look neat, well groomed, and put together. A business suit is always a safe bet, especially if you are facing clients. But wearing a suit that looks like you slept in it doesn't do much for your credibility. Make sure to wear clothes that fit properly and are pressed and free of wrinkles and stains. Dress for the job you *want*, not the job that you *have,* but don't take this too far (you shouldn't out-dress your boss). Also, try to dress within your salary range.

In one sense, women are lucky because our range of clothing options is much broader than that of men. Yet, while we have more dressing choices, we also have more room for missteps. If people are focusing on your clothes for the wrong reasons, then you're probably wearing the wrong clothes. Find a professional style in which you are comfortable because it will give you the greatest degree of confidence.

The dress code on Wall Street is still conservative, even though most firms have implemented an everyday business casual dress code or casual Fridays. Casual dress opens a new realm of clothing options, as well as a whole new slew of possibilities for fashion faux pas. Summer is a particularly notorious time of the year when the formality of office attire tends to diminish. Always think about what your outfit is saying about you.

Casual attire aside, personal grooming is *never* acceptable in the personal space of a cubicle or on the trading floor. Personal grooming, such as clipping your fingernails or brushing your hair, should be done in a private space like a bathroom, and only if it's a mid-day touch up. If it's part of your morning routine, then it's best to do it at home before you come to the office. I frequently see young women changing their hairstyles throughout the day. In the morning, their hair is down; by lunch, it's in a ponytail; by 3 o'clock, it's in a bun with a pencil sticking out of it. Do your hair once, and then leave it alone. And please, do not play with your hair in meetings. As a side note, constantly playing with your hair is a stress-related condition and can signify anxiety, incompetence, uncertainty and shyness.

How you arrive at work leaves you open to all sorts of judgments and interpretations. How you prepare for work tells people how prepared you are for the job and how serious you are about the position. It also speaks to your sense of reliability. Coming to the office with wet hair doesn't give me the impression that you are putting your best foot forward. It gives me the impression that you overslept and are running late for work, which leads to all other kinds of judgments. When I see women consistently putting their make-up on in the bathroom, I can't help but think to myself, "Girl, get it together." Worst of all, these behaviors give me the impression of someone who isn't ready for a promotion.

You don't need to read a company manual to see what *is* and what *is not* appropriate to wear to work. When dressing for the office, the culture of the firm usually sets the standard for the attire, so to get a sense of what to wear, just look around. When I worked at JP Morgan, it was a very conservative bank with a buttoned-up culture. Merrill was more lenient about what was acceptable. As such, women pushed the envelope a bit more, which resulted in inappropriate comments and subsequent lawsuits with charges of harassment. The lesson there is that how you dress will tend to dictate how you are treated.

Here are some common fashion blunders seen around the office:

Too much cleavage –The most common fashion mistake made by women is showing too much cleavage. It's never really appropriate to show any cleavage at work, but too much is an absolute no-no. If your bra is showing, or if your boobs are pouring out of your outfit, then you need a different shirt. Showing too much décolletage is unprofessional and distracting. So, unless you work at Hooters, your boobs should stay in your shirt.

Too much leg – Skirts should be knee-length or longer. Although most professionals would agree that mid-thigh is too short for the office, it is quite popular to wear shorter skirts with tights and flats. But if you wear a shorter skirt, be mindful of your movements so as not to over-expose yourself.

<u>Too much skin</u> – The bare midriff is inappropriate for the office. Sleeveless shirts are up for debate and depend upon the culture of your firm, while spaghetti straps and strappy dresses never make the cut, so save those for the weekends. Keep in mind that the more skin you show, the less seriously people will take you.

<u>Too much makeup</u> – Makeup should be used to highlight your features, not to draw attention to the fact that you're wearing make-up. You don't want to come into the office looking like you're ready to turn tricks.

<u>Too much bling</u> – There is a certain kind of bling that is acceptable on Wall Street, and it usually comes with a marriage proposal. Jewelry should complement your outfit, not overpower it. Remember, you're not Beyoncé.

<u>Exposed tattoos</u> – Tattoos have grown enormously popular, and it seems that young people are more likely to have them than not. However, in a conservative firm they are still unprofessional, so keep your tats under wraps - *especially the tramp stamps or anything potentially offensive.*

Inappropriate shoes – Shoes fall into a gray area, and defining the margin of what is considered appropriate depends upon the culture of your firm. Shoes that are too sexy or risqué are inappropriate for work no matter which Wall Street firm you work for. Flip-flops are also never acceptable. The gray area comes into play with the open toe. Some cultures frown on the open toe, while others deem it to be acceptable. In a speech given to the JP Morgan training program, professionalism expert Marjory Brody offered the guideline that if you do wear open-toed shoes, your feet should be pedicured and your toes should be polished. I happen to agree with Ms. Brody on this one and believe that there is nothing less appealing than a pair of unkempt feet.

Equally as important as the condition of your feet is the condition of your shoes. Shoes that are scuffed, with heels and soles that are beaten or worn out, generally make a poor impression and speak to your attention to detail. Many Wall Street firms have shoe shine guys that come to the trading floor, so there shouldn't be any reason for shoes to be kept in poor condition. Shoes are an enormously important fashion accessory; more people are looking at your shoes than you think. So do pay close attention to your shoes.

All this may seem quite obvious, yet there are plenty of examples of inappropriate dress around the office. And if you think that none of this matters in a world as image conscious as

Wall Street, then you may be making some missteps yourself. Entrepreneur Mark Zuckerberg was absolutely slammed by Wall Street analysts after wearing his signature hoodie to investor meetings during Facebook's IPO[3] roadshow. It was thought to be a sign of immaturity and disrespect. His ability to be CEO of Facebook also came into question. Obviously, everything worked out just fine for Zuckerberg, and Facebook became the largest IPO in technology history, but this took the focus off of his company and created a lot of unwanted noise. The first rule of sales is that you never want to give your prospective customers any reason to be uncomfortable with you before you have even started selling your product. And make no mistake: in a corporate environment, you are always selling yourself and your brand. Dressing professionally is an important part of your brand and it is seen as a reflection of your attitude. To put your best foot forward and dress for success, I suggest investing in at least one nice suit and two pairs of good quality shoes. And to ensure that your look is complete and that you haven't forgotten any critical pieces of your wardrobe, like I did that day, you should consider the purchase of a full-length mirror.

---

[3]  IPO stands for Initial Public Offering, which is the process by which a private company goes public and makes their stock available for purchase by the public on an exchange.

# WHAT ISN'T SAID

**I ALWAYS FELT THAT** it was important to listen more than I spoke. As a result, I had a keen ability to intently hear what clients wanted and needed. The mistake that I made was that I didn't listen to what wasn't being said. I focused on the content of the message and paid little to no attention to body language, which has its own dialect. Body language can portray more information than the spoken word because your subconscious actions reveal your thoughts without conscious manipulations. It is important to also know that every single gesture that you make creates an impression and contributes to an overall opinion that is formed about you. Research suggests that it only takes three seconds for a person to decide whether or not they like you. Some of the slightest cues, which you may disregard as insignificant or irrelevant, could have an impact on the impressions that you are making.

Take the handshake for example. This small gesture makes a huge impression when it comes to forming judgments about what you are like as a person, as well as a professional. A handshake is so important that even my mother, who wasn't a businessperson, knew its value. I distinctly remember her telling me that she disliked someone based on how they shook her hand. She then taught me proper handshake technique, which includes a firm grip (but not too firm), direct eye contact (for the entire duration of the handshake), and a smile. The proper handshake says that you are confident and self-assured, while a smile adds an uplifting tone to the greeting. Practice if you need to, but be sure to get it right, because you can't undo a first impression and it is an essential detail.

I am always surprised, about how blatantly unaware people are of their physical actions, as I observe their posture and behaviors around the office. Just the other day, I watched in horror and disgust as my young colleague picked his teeth during a meeting. And he didn't just pick one tooth; he practically stuck his whole fist into his mouth to perform a dental cleaning. I actually had to kick him under the table to get him to stop. Another common body language blunder is in the choice of locations where people decide to either chat with their friends or to text. For some reason, people think that it is ideal to wait, chat, or text in front of doorways, at the top of escalators, or at the bottom of stairs – so pay attention and move out of the way!

Body language includes all of your non-verbal communication, and it speaks more loudly than your words. Body language offers clues, many times unintentional clues, about what you are thinking and what you are feeling. And often times what you are THINKING and what you are FEELING may be different than what you are actually SAYING. This is why it is so important to be mindful of your body language. You always want your actions to match your words – otherwise, people won't trust you and will think you're full of shit. I learned this all too well after being jilted by a guy whose elusive behavior was unmatched by his proclamation of love for me. He told me that I was "The One" and then he disappeared and wouldn't return any of my phone calls. My friend Chong summed it up perfectly with this advice: "Don't listen to a man's words, listen to his actions." He was referring to situations of love, but the same does apply to business as well.

When I think about intuitive intelligence, I categorize the understanding of body language into three distinct skill levels that I uninventively dubbed levels 1.0, 2.0, and 3.0. Level 1.0 is the basic awareness of body language. Comprehension at this level would raise your sensitivity to physical gestures and would allow you to read common cues. At this level, you also become cognizant of your own body language and the messages that you are sending with your actions. Once you've grasped the concepts of this level, you would instinctually advance to Level 2.0. At this level you would develop the skills needed to detect discrepancies between words and actions. This is a nifty skill to have not only in the business world but also in personal relationships. Essentially, Level 2.0 boosts your bullshit radar. Level 3.0 is much more advanced, so I will leave it for further discussion later in this chapter.

All your behaviors and behavioral patterns work together in concert to create your brand. Body language is a science and one worthy of study because it is a key factor in achieving greater success. When properly used, body language can help you develop positive business relationships, influence people, and help you present ideas with greater impact. It is a critical factor in establishing credibility, building trust, and projecting confidence.

Let's now look at Level 1.0, which consists of the basics of body language. I've outline some of the most common cues below, along with the interpretation of what your body language is saying.

| The Action | What your body language says | The Fix |
|---|---|---|
| Slouching posture with your hands propping up your head and your elbows on the table | Says that you are bored, disinterested, and disengaged | Standing tall, shoulders back, feet firmly planted, and chin up. When sitting, sit straight up with your back against the back of the chair and your feet, flat on the floor. This tells me that you are confident and engaged. Leaning forward slightly also shows me a greater level of involvement in the conversation. Proper Posture conveys a confident and authoritative presence. |
| Yawning | Tells me that you are tired or bored | Yawning never says anything positive, so please don't ever yawn in a meeting. |
| No eye contact | Tells me that you either lack confidence or that you're lying; it can also be a sign of disrespect | Always look people in the eyes when speaking to them and allow them to look into yours. Looking people in the eyes tells them that you are engaged, interested, and most importantly, honest. It can make or break your presence as it conveys confidence, engagement, and trust. |

| | | |
|---|---|---|
| Crossed arms | Tells me that you aren't open to ideas and that you are defensive | Make a conscious effort not to cross your arms because it gives off a feeling of hostility, particularly when receiving feedback. This especially applies to any contentious discussions. |
| Rolling your eyes | This could mean you disagree with whoever is speaking or that you dislike the person. Either way, it is rude and disrespectful and if you are caught rolling your eyes, you will likely insult the person who is speaking. | Be mindful of all your facial expressions and be sure they match the words that you are speaking. |
| Quiet speech | Quiet speech can have multiple meanings. It can tell me that you are unsure of yourself. It can also be a way of asserting your leadership and strength. And often when leaders speak quietly, it forces the audience to intently listen without making a move. You will need to decide which approach you are taking. | If your quiet speech is due to insecurity, you will need to speak up and speak with confidence! Exhale and then take a deep breath before you are about to talk. Use the energy of your breath to help set the volume. Practice speaking from your diaphragm, not from your throat. |

| | | |
|---|---|---|
| Crackling voice | Tells me that you are nervous or unsure of yourself | The crackle of your voice will go away with experience and knowledge of the subject matter. The more you know about the topic, the more confident and comfortable you will become when speaking in front of an audience. Strength of voice can remove the crackle; this requires speaking from your diaphragm. |
| Daydreaming | Tells me that I don't have your full attention and that you are bored | Stay focused on the conversation by looking people in the eyes. |
| Limp handshake | Gives me the impression you are weak and tells me that you lack confidence and aren't sure of yourself | Always offer a firm grip but don't linger – that's just creepy. |
| Biting your nails | This is a sign of stress, frustration or nervousness. | If you are a nail biter, try and keep your nails manicured and polished. Polish can deter this unappealing habit. |
| Playing with your hair | This has many meanings ranging from stressed and anxious to insecure. How you play with your hair can change the meaning – for example, twirling your hair is a sign of flirting | Be cognizant of the message you are sending by playing with your hair and be sure it is indeed the message you want to send i.e. you may not want to twirl your hair in a meeting. |

| Taking notes | Taking notes shows that you think what the speaker is saying is important. This also shows that you are engaged and focused on the discussion | It is important when you are starting in your career that you attend every meeting with a notebook so that you seem prepared. Whenever anyone comes to a meeting without a pen and a notebook, I have a hard time taking them seriously unless they are very senior, in which case they are expecting everyone else to take notes. |

In the game of poker, there is something called a tell, but I have found that it doesn't only apply to poker. A tell is a subtle, yet detectable change in a player's behavior or demeanor that gives clues to that player's assessment of their hand. They say that your tell is truer than you are. Because a tell is unconscious, most people are completely unaware of it, and it gives them away every time. My ex-husband used to have a tell, which revealed itself right before he was going to lie. He later asked me how it was that I always knew when he was lying. I told him about his tell. Once he became aware of his tell, he worked to change it, but as a result, he developed another tell. I kept that one to myself.

While body language plays an important role in brand building, its value transcends far beyond that. It is also a useful skill when transacting in business. When I was a young associate in investment banking, I was in a client meeting with the banking team for a deal that we thought we had already won. The meeting went extremely well and by the end, everyone was joking and backslapping. As the meeting broke up, I told the company's CEO that I would urgently send the engagement letter to him for his signature. He paused slightly; then he smiled, nodded his head, and shook my hand. I thought nothing of it, but in a taxi on the way back to the office, my banker said to me, "This deal isn't going to happen." I was shocked and said, "You're crazy! That meeting went so well." But something about the pause and the calculated smile seemed to give my banker cause for concern. He told me that he has been doing this job for such a long time that he'd learned how to accurately read people and situations. He had become so astute that he no longer needed to rely on what people said. I thought he was just being cynical. When we got to the office, I urgently put the engagement letter together and sent it over to the CEO of the company. I followed up with several phone calls but was unsuccessful in making contact. His assistant assured me that he received the letter, but he didn't return any of my calls and never sent back a signed letter. Later that week, it was announced that Morgan Stanley had won the Sole Lead Advisor role on the deal. My banker was right.

Now, let's move along to Body Language Level 3.0, which really isn't about your body at all. It is about your energy. Because we are talking about non-verbal communication, I will define energy as the ethereal extension of your body language. Energy is a universal life force, but it is controversial because it is spiritual in nature. Skeptics doubt its very existence and therefore its consequences and impact come into question, but I believe that is real; it is as real as electricity.

Learning how to properly channel your energy opens you up to entirely new realms of possibilities and becomes a powerful tool. When I reviewed the lost banking deal in my head, I analyzed the exchange of body language cues and concluded that they were almost too subtle to even notice. Yet, my banker picked up on them. I don't even remember him paying such close of attention to the participants in the meeting. I later started to observe him in other interactions and realized that he wasn't always reading body language, but instead, he was reacting to the energy brought into the situation. I found this to be very interesting and so I pursued to seek greater understanding.

I learned that everything in this universe, including you, is made of energy, and all the energy of the universe is interconnected. Your energy is contagious, and it has the power to affect other people's energy. We are constantly in a state of energy exchange, whenever we are in the presence of another. If you are sensitive to the energetic state of the universe, then you are probably already aware of this and know exactly what I am talking about. But for those who don't, think about when someone comes into your space in a bad mood. They don't necessarily say a word, but suddenly your own mood sours and you don't even know why or how it happened. The person's energy collides with your energy and wraps you in a blanket of energetic negativity, which you then carry and spread onto others. Some people have stronger energy than others with an ability to bring down an entire room full of people. Consequently, those same people have the power to elate an entire room. With that type of capability also comes responsibility. Oprah Winfrey has a sign in her dressing room that says "Please take responsibility for the energy you bring into this space."[4] I have long agreed with this and believe that we all should take responsibility for the energy that we carry because it transfers onto others. We can do this through mindfulness. The energy you possess is a choice; with a slight mind shift, you can alter the state of your energy. You can choose to make your impact on the world a positive one or a negative one — that is up to you. But keep in mind that negative people tend to repel positive people and attract negative circumstances. As I said earlier, energy is contagious. When you associate with negative people, their energy rubs off on you. They infect both your energy and your headspace and then you have the potential of becoming negative yourself. This has a greater tendency of occurring if you keep frequent company with negative people. That is why it is sometimes necessary to disconnect yourself from those people who carry a toxic perspective. Positive people seem to have a huge light around them as they spread their joy onto others. They make people around them feel at ease and leave a warm and pleasant feeling behind after they've left you. Positive people attract positive things. So, the decision about what kind of person you want to be is entirely up to you. But as we are talking about building a positive brand I hope the answer is obvious.

---

[4]  Quote by Dr. Jill Bolte Taylor

# BIG GIRLS DON'T CRY

**CRYING IS HEALTHY. IT** can bolster the immune system by providing a necessary form of emotional release. It can even make you stronger by boosting feelings of resiliency, while simultaneously strengthening your capacity for empathy. Crying also releases stress. But unless a tragedy has occurred, crying at the office is generally a bad idea. I know Facebook COO Sheryl Sandberg has admitted to having cried in front of her boss Mark Zuckerberg and has publically stated that she believes it is acceptable for women to cry at work. However, let me just point out one thing. Sheryl Sandberg is worth $1.26 billion dollars, so as the song goes, she can cry if she wants to. But for the rest of us who aren't worth a yard[5], I would strongly suggest trying to hold it together in the office.

Crying is stigmatized as a sign of weakness or the inability to handle the pressures of the job. The word "unstable" comes to mind. It is still very much considered a feminine trait that goes hand in hand with our other feminine qualities of being too emotional and moody. When colleagues and bosses believe

---

[5]   *Wall Street slang for billions*

you are too emotional and can't handle the stress of the job, your career will likely suffer. When women cry in the office, it makes everyone around them feel uncomfortable, especially if you are in a leadership position. If you frequently cry at work, you may find yourself to be passed over for promotions or you may miss out on opportunities.

But this is where men and women are physiologically different. Women tend to cry as an involuntary response to trauma. When Hillary Clinton lost the presidential election, she was slammed for not delivering her concession speech on the same night that she lost. Most said that it was a double standard. Perhaps it was, but when I put myself in her shoes, I knew that I would have never have been able to deliver that speech either. It made me think back to the day my father died. I was so distraught that I couldn't even speak. My brothers didn't have anywhere near the same physical response that I did, but they didn't love my father any less. It is just that women are different than men and so we don't respond in the same manner. Crying is natural, but it doesn't belong in the office. If you need to cry, try to find a private place where you won't be seen.

Most women have cried in the office at one time or another. Whether it was because of a stressful meeting, a terrible boss, or a fight with a co-worker, most of us have cried at least once. In my personal life, I am far more emotional than in my professional life. I do, however, admit that at times, I have gotten so wrapped up in the intensity of the moment that I couldn't help but to shed a tear (or to sob uncontrollably as the case may be). But I can count the number of times that have I cried in the office on one hand; it was exactly twice. The first time was a long time ago and it was after six months of being berated by my yelling and screaming boss. The second time was much more recently and I can still feel the sting of the moment.

In September of 2008, Merrill Lynch was saved from the brink of collapse by a merger with Bank of America. At the end of that year, when Wall Street prepared to pay bonuses to its employees, we expected our bonuses to be decreased because of our poor financial performance, *to say the least*. By this time, I had left my role in HR and had been working in the business for several years. The business at Merrill was a boys club and my supervisor at the time, was a "good ole boy," as they say. He was also slippery and I feared that he was going to use the bonus money that had been earmarked for me to pay his inner circle. I sensed his plan all along, especially when he started mentioning how bad the bonus pool was. But my HR colleagues told me a different story. They said that Merrill's CEO was able to convince the BoA CEO to pay adequate bonuses to ensure retention of talent. So, I warned my other bosses and asked them to keep an eye on the situation. But with the merger dust not yet settled, my other bosses had other distractions. In the end, my total comp was down by 80%. Ughhh, that was a blow to the gut and it hurt.

What made the situation even worse was the way in which my supervisor delivered the bonus message. It's never enough for your boss to just give you the shaft; for some reason, they feel compelled to feed you a load of crap in the process. I refer to this as the bonus foreplay, because they seem to kiss you and fondle you before they fuck you. This only adds insult to injury. During my bonus foreplay, I was sitting across the table from my boss when he tried to sell me on the idea that this bonus amount wasn't really that bad. But my face was stoic and he could tell that I wasn't buying his first serving of bullshit. Then, in a pitiful attempt to try and elicit sympathy, he told me a pathetic story about his own personal financial woes. This is generally bad form because most bosses make more than their subordinates. In my particular case, my boss was a twenty-five year veteran of the bond business and probably earned two-three bucks[6] a year. I made a mere fraction of his salary and I relied heavily on my bonus money in order to pay my bills. I was disgusted by the whole situation and I couldn't wait to get out of the room and away from him. I don't even think that he had finished talking by the time I got up and left.

I ran back to my office, which was near the prop-trading desk. I was sobbing uncontrollably when one of the prop traders barged in, just as he always did. That day, however, was very different. I don't think he ever regretted anything more than walking into my office. He was concerned because I was crying so hard. He asked what had happened and I could barely answer through my hyperventilating whimpers - *which were downgraded from the sobs that he heard when he first walked in.* He tried to be compassionate, but boy was he uncomfortable. He kept a far distance from me and didn't even try to cross the line drawn by my desk. He could barely even make eye contact with me as he uttered his empty words of support. His eyes fluttered back and forth between the ceiling and the floor; every once in a while, he glanced over at me to see if I was still crying. Tears, make-up, and snot were all running down my face. It was not a pretty sight and not my finest moment. Then I mustered up the strength to bellow out, "Please leave!" So he got the hell outta

---

[6]  Wall street slang for millions

there. Even though he was trying to be supportive, he did us both a favor by leaving, because neither of us wanted to be there, in that moment. *A few weeks later he asked me out. He said that he developed feelings for me when he saw me cry and that my vulnerability that day was very sexy.* So the lesson here is that while crying is not great as a career strategy, it's not terrible as a dating strategy.

Forty-one percent of women said they have cried at the office, as compared to nine percent of men. When the pressure is on, and stakes are high, or when fatigue and exhaustion set in, it can be difficult to keep your emotions in check. As I said, this can result in outbursts, such as crying. If you have a tendency to cry in the office, you can use the following tips to try to help maintain your professional composure.

Pinch yourself: This allows for a small amount of physical pain to distract you and can help prevent tears. Pinch yourself in a sensitive area, like the flesh between your fingers. This is very effective for many people when it comes to preventing crying.

Breathe: Taking deep breaths in through your nose and out through your mouth also can prevent crying. The extra oxygen will give you a bit of a high, which can help soothe you.

Look up: For some reason, looking toward the ceiling can help prevent crying because it will stop the tears from escaping. The tears will usually fall once you put your head back in a regular position.

<u>Walk away</u>: If possible, leave the situation and go for a walk around the block. Putting distance between yourself and the stressor will allow you to gather your composure and cool down your emotions.

And if the problem persists, try:

<u>Behavioral modification</u>: The general idea of behavioral therapy is to pay more attention to problem thoughts and behaviors so that you can find better coping mechanisms. You control your emotional responses. You can become empowered by that control. The more you can embrace this truth, the more successfully you will be able to manage your responses to stressful situations.

Part of presenting an image of reliability and consistency is based on how you manage your emotions. Crying can earn you the title of "unstable," but it's not only tears that can brand you as such; it is also mood swings. This is where women are sometimes less aware of their behaviors. We are emotional beings, and we become more emotional with our body's cycle. While this is a fact, it is not a valid excuse for losing your composure at the office. We need to be particularly careful and keep our emotions in check. After all, when it comes to branding, you want to be thought of for the quality of the work product and not for the quantity of your emotional outbursts.

# HINT AND HOPE

**THE FASTEST WAY TO** get to your destination is to ask for directions. The same applies if your destination is the corner office. This means that you should be clear about your intentions and make your ambitions known to your boss. I can't tell you how many times I've heard women tell me that they were passed up for promotions because their boss didn't know that they wanted a bigger job or a higher title. *Like, why else do you think we're working our asses off, Jackass?* But anyway, in business you need to be clear about what you want; sometimes you need to explicitly ask for it. Women are particularly bad at this. We drop hints and hope that someone will recognize our talent and hard work.

A former colleague of mine worked in our Marketing Department. When her boss resigned, she was the obvious choice for a replacement. As the most senior person remaining, she became the "go to" person for all marketing-related issues. The juniors of the group even looked up to her for direction. She was doing her boss' job but just didn't have the title. Because she kept the day-to-day operations running seamlessly, the company didn't rush to replace her boss either. She was in somewhat of a tough spot; she was taking on all the extra work, but she wasn't empowered because she didn't have the title. She wondered when they were going to finally hire someone to replace her boss, but at the same time, she secretly hoped that they would offer her the job. She asked my advice. To me, this was a no-brainer. "Seize the role," I told her.

To further spell it out for her, I recommended that she have a meeting with management and tell them that she wanted the job. I even gave her a script to prepare her for the meeting. But that meeting never happened because my friend felt too uncomfortable to have that type of direct conversation. Instead, she hinted at her interest and used all sorts of subliminal messaging. A few months later, the company hired a new Head of Marketing. This new boss was hired on as a Managing Director, even though she was a Director in her previous company, which was the same level as my friend. They even both had the same number of years' experience. The job was there for the taking, but my friend lost out on the opportunity because she couldn't ask for what she wanted.

Hinting and hoping rarely yields the desired outcome for your career (or anything else, for that matter). With all the other priorities competing for your boss's attention, you can't trust that they will recognize all your efforts. Even if your boss does recognize your hard work, if you don't clearly communicate your goals and ambitions, they may assume you are not interested in a promotion. This is exactly what happened to my friend. I, for one, would never leave my career up to chance. I do not assume anything. Instead, I make my intentions well known. When women finally ask for what we want, we seem to feel guilty about it. In many ways, women feel that they are undeserving of bigger, better opportunities; we have a hard time asking for a bigger job, a better role, or more money. So, we work harder and hope that someone will notice and recognize us for it by giving us the kiss on the forehead that we are seeking. But it doesn't really work that way. If you don't ask for what you want, you likely won't get it.

How we operate reminds me of how the mothers of my generation ran their households. My mother, God rest her soul, grew up in a time when a woman's opinion didn't really matter and her greatest career option was to get married. She played her role as wife and mother dutifully. She never stepped out or overstepped, and she certainly never complained. She just kept plugging away thanklessly and continued to run our household like a well-oiled machine. Until one day, she died and the machine fell apart. I tell this story not to elicit pity or sorrow, but to draw parallels to women in the workplace. Women tend to work quietly and tirelessly in hopes that someone will notice their efforts. But working quietly is the surest way to guarantee that recognition will never come. Yet, women continue to do this throughout their entire careers until they die—not literally, but until they leave the company or workforce altogether.

Although my generation began to demand greater a balance in the household, we still have a tendency to fall into these traditional roles in the workplace. Women aren't good at asking for we want because we grew up watching our mothers work tirelessly in thankless jobs. We have been socialized to work quietly and diligently behind the scenes or at the side of a man. We weren't taught to ask for what we wanted and we certainly weren't encouraged to assertively go get it. And most importantly we weren't taught that we were deserving of it.

But all this is changing with each new generation. Women are demanding greater equality both at home and in the workplace. Millennial women are by far the more likely to ask for what they want and to express dissatisfaction for what they don't want than women of previous generations. But until the value of women is universally recognized and becomes a visceral part of our society, as <u>evidenced by equal pay</u>, women will continue to think of themselves as worth slightly less than a man.

This is our own deeper psychological issue that we will evolve from over time. But for now, we need to recognize the challenge of our DNA and learn to overcome it. Because its result is behavioral, we can learn new methods. When my new boss became the head of my group, she had just been promoted to Managing Director. When I congratulated her, she told me how difficult it was for her to get that title and that the actual promotion process wasn't easy. In addition to all her hard work that she had already put in to earn the title, she also had to work hard to actually get the title. She told me that she had been passed up for promotions twice. After the second time, she went over her boss's head, to his boss, and demanded an explanation. He told her that her current scope of her role was too narrow and didn't warrant an MD title. So, she insisted that they find her a new role that was large enough to warrant her promotion. This was tricky because there weren't any open roles at the moment. But she was firm and pushed hard, while also being careful not to come across as erratic, emotional or disrespectful. She also knew that she was a valuable asset to a firm that didn't have many senior women. She <u>consistently</u> stayed on top of her request so management knew she wasn't just going to go away or roll over on this matter. After some maneuvering, they opened up a global role for her. The following year, she was promoted to Managing Director.

I particularly like this story because I think she negotiated this masterfully. She struck a balance between asking for what she wanted and protecting her brand. Everyone knew her as one of the nicest people you would ever meet. She was respectful to everyone and used her influence, rather than force, to engage people and never felt the need to pull rank. She proved that it's possible to operate with kindness as long as you also assert yourself when needed. When it came right down to going after what she wanted, she didn't hint and hope. She wasn't afraid to ask for what she wanted because she truly felt that she rightfully deserved it. And this is the key to getting what you want; you have to first wholeheartedly believe that you are worthy and deserving of it. Only then will you go out there and fight for what you want with conviction.

# NEGOTIATING YOUR WORTH

**WHEN ASKING FOR WHAT** you want, you should also include your compensation. If women are bad at asking for what we want when it comes to opportunities, then we are *even worse* about negotiating our monetary worth. During the span of my entire career, I've had some good financial years and some bad ones. The basis for this varied across a spectrum of reasons, including the market environment, poor business performance, and corporate politics. Individual performance is also a factor of compensation. While it is my opinion that performance should be the greatest factor contributing to financial success, I've shared several stories that indicate that isn't always the case.

It is both disheartening and disenfranchising to work hard and not be paid what you believe you are worth. I felt frustrated, knowing that at times, I was paid less than my colleagues that did the same job as me, but not as well. When I was starting out in my career, I complained about this to my Aunt Vera. The advice that she gave me was to simply ask for a raise. With all due respect, I told her that wasn't how things were done at JP Morgan. A discussion about money would have been considered a distasteful practice at a firm, where the employees believed that working there was a privilege. But Aunt Vera called bullshit on this. She said to me, "Negotiations happen everywhere; they happen behind closed doors, and they happen between men." She then went on to convince me that if I wanted to play with the big boys, I'd better learn to ask for what I wanted, *and that included money.* She was absolutely right, on every count.

For starters, negotiations do occur all the time and they take place behind closed doors, which is why we never hear about them. But having worked in HR, I can assure you that those conversations are indeed taking place and they are happening (mostly) between men to negotiate better opportunities for themselves. In my experience, it has been rare to see women negotiate bigger raises and bonuses unless they have an offer in hand from a competitor. Aunt Vera's advice about learning to play with the big boys was also important for me to hear because, in essence, she was telling me to grow up. When it came to negotiating my salary and asking for more money, I did feel like a little girl asking her daddy for money. I needed to overcome this.

Most women are very uncomfortable with having conversations about money, so they avoid them altogether. They fall back on the hint and hope strategy. Actually, most women don't even hint, they just hope. Then when they don't get what they hoped for, they are disappointed. What's worse yet is that in order to protect themselves from disappointment, they lower their expectations and settle for less. But what we, as women, should be doing is learning how to "settle for more."[7] I took Aunt Vera's advice to heart, which began by acknowledging

---

[7] *Settle for More is the title of Fox News Anchor Meghyn Kelly's new book*

that no comp angel was going to come down from the heavens to hand me a windfall of cash. I knew that if I was going to ever get paid the amount of money that I wanted, I was going to have to ask for it myself. I was going to have to have those big boy conversations that I was dreading.

Before I had my first comp discussion, I prepared by tallying a scorecard of wins that I had made throughout the year, while underscoring the importance of my role in executing the business strategy in the coming year. Over time, and with practice, the compensation discussions became easier. Today, I am quite comfortable discussing this topic. *What makes this conversation easier is that Wall Street Management is filled with greedy bastards, all of whom negotiate for that own best interest. So, they aren't surprised when someone tries to negotiate with them – it's all part of the Wall Street game.* I have made this conversation an annual practice, in order to manage my expectations. The timing of this conversation should align with when bonuses are being decided. For most Wall Street firms, this is usually in the fourth quarter, since bonuses are distributed in the first quarter of the New Year. Although every firm varies slightly in their timing, one thing is consistent across firms: once the money is paid, it is too late to negotiate and try to ask for more money.

The compensation structure on Wall Street was fairly transparent up until recent years when government regulations took effect and began impacting the compensation structure of banks. The formula was based on some attribution of these three metrics (1) your performance or PnL[8] (2), the performance of your business, and (3) the overall company performance. The

---

[8] *PnL stands for Profit and Loss*

weighting of each of these individual components varies based on whatever math best suits the company's objective, which is usually to try to pay you less.

> "Senior management's job is to pay people. If they fu\*k a hundred guys out of a hundred grand each, that's a million more for them. They have four categories: happy, satisfied, dissatisfied, and disgusted. If they hit happy, they've screwed up: They never want you happy. On the other hand, they don't want you so disgusted you quit. The sweet spot is somewhere between dissatisfied and disgusted."
>
> — Quote from character Greg Lippman, The Big Short by Michael Lewis

In years where you've killed it, they hose you because the business was down. In years that the business did well, they hose you because the rest of the company did fuck all. So, whichever formula works in the company's favor is the formula they will use to determine your comp. And the moon, the stars, and all the planets have to align in order for you to have a windfall year.

Regardless of the changes in the corporate environment over the last several years, the principles of negotiations remain the same. They are based almost entirely on leverage. A challenging market environment (currently) sets the backdrop for most negotiations in this industry. With talented people willing to work for a fraction of their worth, jobs have been re-priced to pay far less than they once paid. Leverage is tilted in the favor of the companies. All these factors need to be taken into consideration when negotiating your salary and other compensation.

It is also important to have a soberingly realistic idea of the value that you bring to your company, whether or not you can be easily replaced, and at what cost. This includes your perceived value, so if your boss doesn't value what you do, then you won't really have much leverage in the negotiation process. If threatening to quit is your strategy, it may end up backfiring on you, so be careful with that approach. In the current market environment jobs are hard to come by, so it may be best to wait for a market upswing before playing hardball with your career in the balance. Timing is an important factor in negotiating, and sometimes you have to lay low and wait patiently for the right opportunity before striking.

During the dot-com boom of the late 1990s, a soaring economy had talent fleeing Wall Street for opportunities in the Tech Sector. This exodus caused a brain drain that ignited a war for talent among firms and across industries. In the spring of 2000, a first-year analyst wrote a letter to his management at Salomon Brothers that represented the collective views of a pool of 500 or so analysts. His letter included a list of demands as well as suggestions on how the company could improve the treatment of its employees. He specifically highlighted the general mistreatment of analysts, which was ironic because, in the investment-banking world, analysts are at the very bottom of the food chain and have virtually no say in anything. An analyst's life belongs to the banker for whom they work. Their personal lives, which include nights and weekends, belong entirely to the firm.

Included in the list of demands were creature comforts like more meal money, use of the company gym, relaxed dress code, showers, rooms with beds, rec rooms, and even concierge services to handle chores like picking up laundry. The letter and its demands were so shocking that it rattled the ranks of upper management across all of the Wall Street firms. But what was more surprising was the firm's acquiescence to the demands. Management caved. The analysts' demands were met, and all other bulge bracket firms had to follow suit in order to stay competitive. As you can see, it's all about timing and leverage.

As I mentioned earlier, there were times when I suffered some bad financial years, most of which were during times of company acquisitions. Mergers present a unique set of challenges as employees reposition and maneuver to land the one consolidated job that was once two. After one of the big bank mergers, I ended up working for a boss from the other heritage firm. I had several bad comp years under her reign as she didn't like me very much and punished me with whatever power she had. I grew tired of this and decided to find another job within the company. So, I reached out to my mentor and asked for her help. I had always done outstanding work for her and her clients and so she was willing to help me. With her assistance, I began networking and searching for a new role.

A few weeks later, my department underwent a re-organization which put my mentor at the helm. Now, she was my boss's boss. Finally, the tables were about to turn in my favor. After my mentor had settled in, she asked to speak with me about my role in the department. She knew that she needed my help in executing her vision, so I became critical to her success. I viewed this as an opportunity to make up for all the bad comp years that I had endured and I could now recalibrate my value to the market. I agreed to stay and work for her under the condition that I would be properly compensated when bonuses were paid. She wasn't at all surprised by my terms.

A few months passed and it was now August right before compensation discussions began. By this time, I had conducted all the necessary research to benchmark my compensation against industry peers. So, I knew what our competitors were paying for my job. I reminded her of our conversation because, again, managers are busy with their own priorities, and although your comp is at the forefront of *your* mind, it isn't necessarily on top of *your manager's* mind. In this case, she said it was one of her top priorities. I came back to her in September, when the first set of bottom-up figures were submitted to senior management. I continued to check-in just to make sure that she didn't lose sight of the objective. In October, we had our first conversation about real numbers. She gave me an inkling of what she was thinking, and the number was almost double what it had been the previous year. But, I had a number in my head, and that number was a 130% increase. So, when she told me the number my response was, "That's a good start, but it's not enough." I have always been a team player and took many bullets for the team, but not this time. So, I said to her, "Do whatever you have to do, even if it means taking money out of someone else's pocket." My tone was serious and it conveyed a message that my satisfaction was not negotiable. She agreed to fight for more money, but she also couldn't help herself and fell back on the typical management rhetoric of it being a bad year and this being out of her control. I ignored her comment by pretending that I didn't even hear it.

In November, a management memo went out to all employees communicating that poor financial performance would cut bonuses by at least 30% and that there would be no raises. I went to her one last time just to underscore that my expectation was that the content of this memo would not apply to me and that I was one of the few exceptions, *because there always are exceptions.* She agreed. That year, my compensation was up 115%. And although it fell short of the number in my head, I was very happy. A senior HR rep later told me that I received the largest percentage increase out of anyone in the entire firm that year. And although I would have usually thought of her comment as mere lip service, that year I happened to believe her. She also said that I was the topic of many long and contentious management discussions. "Good," I thought to myself. Now all of our management team knows who I am.

The following year, I ended up leaving the firm and my new salary and bonus set the baseline for my compensation package in future negotiations. This set me on course for a much higher earning trajectory. Negotiating your worth is important regardless of where you work, but on Wall Street, it is a normal part of doing business. To reiterate my Aunt Vera's message from many years ago: If you want to play with the big boys, then you'd better learn to ask for what you want. Here a few tips to help you negotiate.

- Do your homework and find out what your job is worth on The Street.
- Come prepared with facts and examples that support your case and illustrate why you deserve a raise in the first place. Employees who demonstrate their contributions to the company are far more likely to succeed in their negotiations.
- Give only one number, not a range, because they will always pay the bottom of the range.
- Get it in writing. Whenever money is at stake, always get it in writing; a promise is not enough.
- Be bold in the delivery of your message. Be sure to convey conviction with your voice and nonverbal cues that can influence the outcome of a negotiation.

And

- When interviewing for a new job, be prepared with your compensation requirements, even at your very first interview. There have been some times when compensation has been brought up earlier than I would have expected, and you always want to stand ready to have that conversation.

# A LOSING BATTLE

**WALL STREET FIRMS ARE** stacked with hierarchies that are protected by protocols and reinforced with ego. Whenever the hierarchical protocol is disrupted, it not only rattles the system, but it also bruises some sensitive egos. At times these hierarchies remind me of high school because Wall Street has its own version of seniors picking on freshmen. Here, analysts and associates are expected to listen to VPs, VPs listen to Directors, and everyone listens to Managing Directors. There is also a chain of command in which you are expected to follow the instruction of your boss. Any violation of this order is perceived as insubordination and bears consequences. A good rule of practice is to simply treat all of your colleagues with respect, regardless of their status or level. That even includes levels below you because it is not uncommon to have someone leapfrog over you through the course of a career and people always remember how you've treated them.

> "I've learned that people will forget what you said, people will forget what you did, but people will never forget how you made them feel.
>
> —Maya Angelou

It also is important to respect the chain of command and to show humility in front of your more senior colleagues. This was obvious to my generation from the moment we set foot in the door. But respect for hierarchy and authority isn't really a characteristic that is typical of Millennials, because they have been raised to treat everyone like peers, including their parents. As such, Millennials have grown up without the ingrained respect for clear boundaries that other generations were taught. And we actually knew this about Millennials before they joined the workforce. We even prepared for this upon their arrival. As such, there is greater tolerance for this now. Even still, Wall Street firms are deeply rooted in rigid protocols, so overstepping or acting with too much familiarity may not bode well. Make sure you tread carefully.

Keep in mind that your manager holds the ultimate power over your career, so getting into a pissing contest with your boss is never a good idea. Your boss has influence over your performance reviews and promotions and decides your compensation. Your boss can also interfere with your mobility within the company, which can limit your career opportunities. A standoff with your boss can get rather ugly because it always seems to come down to a battle of egos, and whenever egos get hurt people become petty, nasty, and vindictive. The sole focus of their mission then becomes winning. Know this: even if it seems like you are the one winning when you are up against your boss, you will lose in the end.

I once had a boss that transferred into the investment bank from retail banking. If you have ever worked in banking, you would know that these two businesses are worlds apart in terms of their culture. Retail banks service what is referred to as "Main Street" customers. These are individuals like you and me who many need banking services such as a checking or savings account. Investment banks provide financing and investment opportunities to institutions like corporations, other banks, or institutional investors such as asset managers, hedge funds or pension funds. The size of the transactions run in the millions, if not in the billions, and the complexity of the products are far greater than those on the retail side. Because the nature of the businesses in an investment bank are far more sophisticated than in retail you could probably imagine that the cultures of each business vary greatly, even within the same company. I would even go so far as to say that the culture of two different investment banks would be more similar than the culture of an investment bank and a retail bank of the same company. Given the backdrop that I have just described, you might also gather that a supervisor from retail would have difficulty succeeding in a role as a supervisor in an investment bank; they likely don't understand the products and there is an enormous cultural divide.

I myself struggled to work for a boss who came from the retail side of the house and was frustrated by her rudimentary product knowledge and unwillingness to learn the business. Whenever she spoke, I rolled my eyes and was completely disinterested in what she had to say. The level of my intensity also seemed to clash with her lackadaisical approach. Our personalities mixed like oil and water. I reached a point where I began to circumvent her altogether and even omitted her from meetings that she expressed interest in attending. Furthermore, I bashed her behind her back. As a result, the business thought she was a joke and didn't take her seriously. I thought that I was so much smarter than her, but in the end, that didn't matter. That year, my comp suffered dramatically and she almost fired me – and although she didn't, she would have had every right to do so. Ultimately, I paid a hefty price for my behavior and the cost was greater than the gratification to my ego.

Challenging your boss in private is one thing, but it is entirely different when you do it in front of others. And if you think that undermining your boss in the presence of others makes you look smarter, then you'd better think again. To others who observe this, it comes across as immature and unprofessional. It is also uncomfortable to witness. Most bosses will not tolerate being made a fool of and they likely will retaliate in some way. Bashing your boss behind their back is even worse than challenging them in front of others. And this is true not just on Wall Street but in any industry. Just look what happened when highly decorated Iraqi War General Stanley McChrystal made disparaging remarks about our Former Commander and Chief, President Barack Obama. For General McChrystal, this was one losing battle, and it will be for you too.

# IT IS A POPULARITY CONTEST

**EVERYONE WANTS TO BE** "liked." While Millennials tend to measure their popularity through social media and the number of Instagram followers they have, we have all fallen victim to the pressures of social status at some point in our lives. Think back for a moment to high school. For many of us, it was a time that we'd rather forget, a stressful time, in which we struggled to somehow fit it under mounting social pressure. It was also an unforgiving time when one misstep could get you banished from your social circle and tarred and feathered for everyone to see...*and of course to laugh*. It was also a time when you first learned the value of name-dropping and when becoming popular was a matter of getting into the right clique. Well, Wall Street is pretty much like high school on steroids. Who you know can open doors to all sorts of opportunities, and one false career move could have you blacklisted forever.

On Wall Street, getting in the door can still be about who you know. Even though most firms recruit from top-ranked universities, being at the top of your class alone may not be enough to land you the job. When I worked in Recruiting, I can't tell you how many resumes came across my desk labeled as "Must Hire" because the candidate had some personal connection to someone high up in the ranks of the organization. These candidates were rarely deserving of an interview, let alone qualified to land a job, yet somehow they were always hired. Some of these candidates were adequate, but many of them were of such poor quality that I often wondered if they were even competent enough to bring me a cup of coffee. Depending on how bad the candidate was, I would sometimes push back and try to convince the individual that hiring the candidate was not in the best interest of the firm. Truth be told, they were also doing a disservice to the candidate, because the odds of them failing were far greater than their odds of them succeeding. Often times, they wouldn't even make it out of the gate and would fail out in the training program.

Once you assert that you can actually do the job and do it well, it is also important to be liked. It is human nature to want to be around people we like, especially if you are spending 40/60/80 hours a week with them. There is nothing more stressful that working with someone who has a difficult or prickly personality. If you are such a person, you should already know it. By the time you become an adult, someone should have told you this already. If you aren't sure, then now may be a good time for some introspection and it may also behoove you to become just a little bit nicer. This will help increase your likeability factor, and believe me, it will go a long way in helping your career.

When I ran the Training Programs, it didn't take very long to figure out who the rotten apples of the bunch were, and in a class of hundreds of trainees, there were quite a few. Usually, by the third day, I would have to deliver what I referred to as the "asshole speech." The speech began like this. "In business, it's not enough to be smart; you also have to be likable. No one wants to work with an asshole, so don't be an asshole...." The speech continued and some would get the message, while others did not. Those who didn't would continue being assholes and would also become a management nightmare. Then one day, they would become managers, at which point they would graduate to become a full-fledged Dick or Biach.

## Habits of the Most Likeable People
## By Napoleon Hill

- They develop a positive mental attitude and let it be seen and felt by others
- They always speak in a carefully disciplined, friendly tone
- They pay close attention to someone speaking to them
- They are able to maintain their composure in all circumstances
- They are patient
- They keep an open mind
- They smile when speaking with others
- They know that not all their thoughts need to be expressed
- They don't procrastinate
- They engage in at least one good deed a day
- They find a lesson in failure rather than brood over it

- They act as if the person they are speaking to is the most important person in the world
- They praise others in a genuine way without being excessive
- They have someone they trust point out their flaws

The reason these assholes are able to become managers in the first place is that they have proven their value in some way. On Wall Street, this way is usually through their PnL, which is the most quantifiable measure of their value. It is also the only qualifier that grants you permission to stay an asshole because the one factor that trumps the asshole quotient is greed. If you're an asshole, but you make a lot of money for your firm or your clients, the odds are high that you and your poor behavior will be tolerated. As such, there are a lot of assholes on Wall Street.

PnL is the most important qualifier of your value. But your PnL is only good while it lasts. One day when the market moves against you, and I promise you that it will *because it always does at some point,* you will find yourself on the wrong side of the trade. Amongst mounting losses, the only thing that may save you is your likeability factor. If you find yourself in the precarious position of having lost money for the firm and being broadly disliked, you may come to face your demise. You will find that when you are standing close to the edge of the cliff staring down at the precipice, someone may just give you a little push because nothing draws sharks out of the water like a little blood.

When it comes to PnL, not everyone can be a top producer, nor does everyone work in a revenue-generating role. If your role isn't directly tied to PnL, proving your value can be a challenge. Always think like a producer and look for ways to measure your accomplishments. It's also important to market your accomplishments so the right people know about them. In the end, if your manager doesn't know what you do then it doesn't matter how good you are because they won't recognize your value.

While self-promotion is one way to make your accomplishments known, a more effective way is to have someone speak on your behalf, like a sponsor. A sponsor is someone senior who takes an interest in your career and looks out for you within the organization. It is a relationship that usually forms organically, based on mutual interests. The reason that someone even becomes your sponsor is because you have banked some good will by doing a good job for them along the way. A sponsor can help get your name out there so you'll be considered for any positions that may arise within your organization. Having the right senior support can clear your pathway to success. A sponsor can also help you get a job in another firm, because when senior people leave they tend to bring in their own teams. A sponsor can provide you with career opportunities while they have a vested interest to help you succeed. You can also help the sponsor in delivering their vision, so in essence, you would be helping your sponsor succeed as well.

Here is a classic example of sponsorship seen through the historic actions of Jamie Dimon.[9] Prior to his current role as CEO of JP Morgan Chase, Jamie was the young protégé of

---

[9]    *Tearing Down the Walls* by Monica Langley

Sandy Weill, the man who built the Citicorp Empire through mega-mergers. Jamie helped Sandy build this behemoth by assembling his own team of smart, talented, and loyal individuals whom he sponsored and promoted. Although Jamie was like a son to Sandy, the relationship between them deteriorated, and in its final culmination, Sandy fired Jamie. Many of Jamie's loyalists objected to his ouster and at least one even quit in protest. Jamie rewarded them with leadership positions when he took the top job as CEO of BankOne, a midsized regional bank headquartered out of Chicago. Jamie laid low for several years, away from the white-hot spotlight of Wall Street, and waited for the right opportunity to stage his comeback. That opportunity came in the form of a merger between JP Morgan Chase and BankOne. Jamie brokered the deal that would one day vault him to the top spot of the largest US bank. This also guaranteed prominent positions for all of Jaime's loyalists that he had collected throughout the years; including Steve Black, the man who himself resigned when Jaime was fired. Black, was already at JP Morgan as the Head of Equities but was rumored to be on the ropes before Jamie came in and elevated him to the co-head of the Investment Bank.

Your ability to recover from adversity may depend upon how you've treated people throughout your career. If you have treated people well, they will watch your back. If you've mistreated them and constantly shit on them, then they will look to bring you down the first chance they get. When your popularity does begin to sink, you will find out who your friends really are. Your enemies will light the match that will begin to singe your popularity, while those who truly hate you will pour gasoline until your career ignites into flames. Once you become persona non grata, you become toxic and no one will want to be associated with you. You will even lose your sponsor's support faster than you could say, "Lance Armstrong."

These are some of the lessons that I learned from the trenches of Wall Street throughout the span of my career. At Merrill, I truly did learn the importance of popularity and saw the difference in my career when I was liked and admired by my colleagues compared to when I wasn't. I left Merrill to follow my sponsor to yet another Wall Street bank, which had a challenging culture that wasn't a good fit for him. He was broadly disliked, and his style was misunderstood. I became equally unpopular, just because of my affiliation with him. After only two short years, my boss resigned from the company leaving me to fend for myself. Before he resigned, I called my friend Chong and said, "My boss is going to quit on Monday, and I'll be fired by Wednesday." But the week went by, and I wasn't fired. Instead, I had the opportunity to retrench and find my new footing. I also had a stroke of luck when three senior guys needed something that only I knew how to do. I was able to prove I had some value. That week, I overheard two of the senior traders talking about me in Spanish. "¿Qué vas a hacer con ella?" one trader asked, as he nodded his head in my direction. The other responded thoughtfully, "Ella puede tener algún valor, así que creo que voy a mantenerla por ahora." Phew, what a relief! I thought they were going to take me out back and shoot me, but instead, I was spared.

When a senior ousting occurs, the new management gets rid of the old guard and they bring in their own team. This is done to ensure the team they have in place is loyal to them and that there isn't a Judas in the bunch. The fatal mistake that my boss made was that he didn't completely clean house while he underestimated how much he was disliked. He naïvely believed that he could win over the team that remained. But loyalties tend to die hard, and his newly inherited team never came around. When I noticed signs of insubordination, I advised my boss that he needed to swiftly fire a few key people and then the rest would fall in line. But he wanted to be liked and believed they would eventually warm to him. They never did, and it ended in his resignation from the firm. When I first joined the firm, I observed an aggressive culture and I instinctually laid low. I drew from the lessons that I learned at Merrill and built alliances first, even before trying to deliver results. I didn't push people around and I leveraged my relationship with my boss to benefit others, not for my own gain or advancement. In other words, I used what power and influence I had for good. I tried not to piss anyone off like I had done in previous jobs and so I kept my own asshole quotient low. This all served me well.

Sponsorship is valuable, but success also hinges on getting the proper advice and guidance. Navigating corporate politics can be challenging. It's always good to draw lessons from those who have more experience than you. Experience is the greatest teacher, but not everyone has the benefit of first-hand experience, particularly when you are promoted into a senior role at very young age. That is when having a mentor could be useful. Good mentors will share their insights based on their own experiences that you can then apply to your own situation. The best mentor-mentee relationships form organically, and those tend to be long lasting. Formal mentor programs that connect a mentor with a mentee can feel very contrived, and I've never observed a program that worked with any consequential level of success.

I already demonstrated how managing up could benefit your career; managing down has its value as well. Juniors tend to be plugged into the vibe of the organization, while seniors tend to sit in their ivory towers and frequently become out of touch with the masses. Staying connected to juniors keeps your fingers on the pulse of what's going on. They also do the lion's share of the work and know how to get things done within the organization. Juniors are also glad to be of assistance to a more senior person. And finally, juniors don't stay juniors forever. They get promoted and could even surpass you through the ranks. If you treat them well they will remember you favorably. Always respect your relationships and don't underestimate their value because one day they may pay off.

> "Never burn bridges. Today's junior prick, tomorrow's senior partner."
>
> —Katherine Parker
> *Working Girl,* the Movie

Relationships with Personal Assistants ("PAs") also have tremendous value, as PAs tend to hold a special kind of power. I have witnessed their influence damage people's careers. Most senior managers have a very close relationship with their PAs. If a PA is mistreated, she would certainly have the ear of her boss, and most bosses do not take kindly to hearing that you have abused their PAs. There may be repercussions for this.

Relationships are paramount in all industries, which is why networking is so important. Networking is an art. But networking events, for the sole purpose of networking, have little value to extract. The most effective networks form naturally, just like any real relationships do. They are based on human connections, established through common ground, and are nurtured through quality time spent together. That is why events such as golf outings and off-sites serve as effective platforms for networking. Once a relationship is formed, make it a point to stay connected. I used to be much better at this than I am today. When the social media site LinkedIn was first created, I was initially reluctant to join, because I was inherently such a great networker. When people would ask me if I was on LinkedIn, my response would always be "I already AM linked in." But my view has since changed and I believe that social media has made it much easier to stay connected and keep track of where people are within the industry. LinkedIn is a powerful tool that helps facilitate that.

As I said, networking is an art; like any art, it takes skill. If forming relationships comes naturally to you, then networking should be second nature. If not, then it can be as painful as a car wreck. The good news is you can improve your relationship-building skills, which are based on connection, empathy, curiosity, and most important listening. If I could name one anti-networking skill, it would be self-absorption. Networking is best done when you don't need anything from anyone. It is better still to network by paying it forward and building good will. Once you have selflessly helped another person, it won't be forgotten. Those whom you've helped will become part of your network. Then, when you need something, it's much easier to call in a favor. When you find yourself in a position of need or desperation, it's a bit too late to start networking.

# PARTYING LIKE A ROCKSTAR

**SOCIALIZING IS A FRUITFUL** way to bolster client and colleague relationships and therefore it is an essential part of doing business. And although the pomp of events and parties has tempered over the years and widespread debauchery has subdued, pockets of excessive behavior still do exist. Company tolerance, however, has diminished, yielding severe consequences for misbehavior. That being said, bad behaviors still occur, especially whenever any mind-altering substances are added to the mix. I remember at my old firm, at least half a dozen employees would be fired each year after the holiday office party for some type of misconduct. Think before you act so that doesn't happen to you.

Office social functions provide a unique opportunity for face time that can help further develop relationships with your clients and colleagues. Removing yourselves from the office and switching to a more relaxed setting helps cultivate team bonding, so I would highly encourage it. And although your participation may not be mandatory, if your boss is attending, you should consider it to be a command performance event. If your boss is *hosting*, you need to be there. Not attending without a good reason can lead to the perception that you are disinterested in your career or that you are unwilling to go the extra mile. Now that you've been invited, use the opportunity wisely and don't turn something positive into a negative.

Work events are almost always paired with drinking because alcohol fosters social bonding by improving your mood and reducing self-consciousness. But alcohol also impairs judgment, which can lead to social mistakes. Losing control of yourself creates the potential for embarrassing situations that could leave lasting impressions on your reputation and cause damage to your career. Always bear in mind that the intent of drinking at a work event is to enhance your social skills and not to get drunk. Learning how to drink responsibly is a bit of a skill, not like Excel or PowerPoint, but more of a life-skill that develops with experience. The first lesson is to understand what kind of drinker you are. This may not be as easy as it seems because sober introspection is required for self-awareness and it is difficult to see yourself, if you are inebriated. Here are some of the different types of drinkers that tend to leave negative impressions:

**The Chatty Cathy:** Do you tend to talk too much? While alcohol helps the flow of conversation, you don't want to tell-all and divulge personal or professional information that may not be appropriate. Keep secrets in the vault where they belong.

**Solution:** Think before you speak. Take a deep breath, then talk.

**The Guzzler:** Do you tend to drink quickly and slam them back?

**Solution:** Learn to sip rather than guzzle. Pace yourself by alternating drinks with glasses of water or order a drink you dislike so you will nurse it all night.

**The Slurrer:** Do you slur your words after just a few drinks? This is particularly bad because your head might be clear, but your speech makes you sound drunk.

**Solution:** You can try and take nootropics, which stimulate brain function. I personally have no experience with them, so I would suggest researching this option.

**The Sloppy Drunk:** Not only does the Sloppy Drunk slur every other word, but they also degenerate into a wreckage of spilled alcohol and vomit; barely standing and stumbling when they walk, the Sloppy Drunk falls all over the place. It's a mess.

**Solution:** If you can't control yourself, you should consider avoiding alcohol altogether. Order a cranberry and soda water with a squeeze of lime. You'll have a delicious drink to hold all night and nobody will be the wiser.

**The Weeper:** Are you a sad drunk? Do you tend to get emotional and cry?

**Solution:** Make arrangements with a friend or close colleague ahead of time to take you out of the party should you start to lose control. *And limit the number of times you ask this favor because, remember, they are still your colleagues, not your babysitters.*

**The Floozy:** For women, this tops the list in terms of the most damaging to your career. The Floozy gets drunk and hooks up with her co-workers and/or clients - you NEVER want to be this girl. Although it is one way to gain popularity around the office, believe me, it's not what you want to be known for and your career will suffer.

**Solution:** Keep your panties on.

**The Mean Drunk:** Do you get contentious or hostile when you drink? Alcohol can increase already aggressive behavior and anger.

**Solution:** Implore self-imposed drinking limits. You may also seek advice from an anger management professional.

Although the heydays of the 80s ended long ago, there is still indecorous behavior that continues to exist within the Wall Street culture. As such, you may find yourself in a predicament where you are asked or offered to partake in illegal drug use. The decision you make is a personal choice, and although I would never judge you, there are definitely people who would. So be careful, because your actions may put your reputation at risk. If your view, however, is one of moral opposition, it is perfectly acceptable to decline participation, but what isn't acceptable is passing judgment onto others. While you should let your moral compass guide your actions, try not to look down on others with righteousness or lecture.

Social missteps while drinking are very common but they shouldn't become a common practice to you. If you happen to get drunk at an office function once, you may likely get a pass. But if it continues, again and again, it will tarnish your brand. You may even find yourself shut out of offices gatherings and left off the guest list for future events. Worse yet, you may become perceived as having a drinking problem and the company may take steps to intervene. If you do think you have a substance abuse problem, you should seek professional assistance, as addiction isn't a battle to be fought alone.

Calling in sick the day after a work event is totally unacceptable and never a good idea. After a night of indulgence, the aftermath should look like it never even happened. Do your best to appear awake, alert, focused and ready to work and not like you're ailing from a hangover. I personally prefer to be the first one in the office the following morning, but if that's too much to ask then just make sure you aren't late and always make sure you come in before your boss does, especially if they were with you the night before. You don't ever want to slither into the office after nine, behind dark sunglasses, and reeking of booze. Although Wall Street types are notorious for playing hard, when it comes to the job, there is still an expectation that commands optimal performance. Even after a night of overindulgence, you still need to show up ready to take on the world. Keep in mind that you are building a career as a finance executive, not as a rock star.

# LOOSE LIPS SINK SHIPS

**WALL STREET RUNS ON** secrets and so the underlying code is discretion. Within the walls of an investment bank, private-side deals are given code names in order to avoid the use of a company's real name. This prevents the suspicions of an impending deal from materially affecting the stock price. Information leaks can jeopardize the execution of an entire transaction with millions of dollars at risk. Your ability to keep matters confidential is not only mandatory for your career success; it's also the law. Any breach of non-public information or any attempt to profit from this information could have severe legal consequences.

> "The most valuable commodity is information."
>
> —Gordon Gekko
> *Wall Street*, the Movie

When you are new to Wall Street, everything is exciting, and working on your first big deal can be such a thrill. It's human nature to want to brag to your friends and family. But you just can't do it. I've heard countless stories through the years of someone just telling their neighbor. A little greed combined with a little hubris and the neighbor calls their broker to put in a trade. Now they've made a few bucks, small potatoes, who cares and who would even notice, right? But before long the SEC[10] will be knocking on your door. They will be able to piece together all the details and create a roadmap that will lead right back to the source of the leak. Don't be that source.

It's important to pay attention when talking on your cell phone, as most people seem completely oblivious. Always be aware of your surroundings when talking about private matters. Pay attention to where you are, what you are saying, and to whom you are speaking. Years ago, I remember sitting next to two people on the ferry who were discussing the prospects of a merger. I heard every word, as did everyone around them. Out of curiosity, I looked up the companies about which they were speaking. I always wondered how many people on that ferry headed to Wall Street did the same thing that I did. I also wondered if anyone traded on that information that day. I can't tell you how many conversations I overhear. Some are of course just gossip, but others are confidential business dealings.

Most twenty-first century businesses are built on highly sensitive information. Aside from confidential data, each industry regards its own information as proprietary and a key differentiating factor that contributes to their competitive advantage. This information could include client lists, business

---

[10] Securities & Exchange Commission – the government agency that regulates the securities markets and maintains fair and orderly function of capital formation in order to protect investors.

plans, operating procedures, organizational charts, proprietary software, and code. Competitor firms are always looking for a leg up, and that sort of information could be useful in undercutting the competition. Sharing that information could not only be disruptive to a company's business, but it could also violate their intellectual property policies.

Confidentiality doesn't only refer to company secrets or what you see within the walls of your office building. Information comes in many forms and is often discovered off premise. New York can be a very small city and it's not uncommon to run into people you know. Being spotted having an innocent drink or dinner with anyone outside of your expected circle can raise all sorts of suspicions. For example, being seen with a former boss or colleague could draw several assumptions, including that you may be discussing your next career move. Random run-ins happen all the time, and when they do, people draw all sorts of conclusions. When the leadership of two companies is seen together, it can ignite mad rumors that could even impact the stock price of the companies. This is why so many meetings take place in private hotel rooms, sometimes even in remote locations outside of the city.

The same applies for meetings within your own firm. I once had a friend and colleague who was the lead contender for a top job as the head of the Equities division. He had a solid relationship with the head of Global Markets, who was also the final decision maker. The two spoke every day, sometimes even several times a day. But one day when my friend tried to call him, his assistant said that he was in a meeting. She knew they were close, so she told him who he was meeting with and said that he worked at another firm. My friend immediately called me and nervously asked me what I thought might be going on. I recognized the name of the person, because I knew him from my previous firm. Not really knowing anything more, I told him that it sounds like they had another contender for the job he was seeking. In my gut, I knew that my friend wasn't going to get that job and I think he knew it too. Later that week, an announcement was made that we had hired a new head of Equities.

The rumor mill on Wall Street is like no other. The less that a company communicates with its employees, the more rampant the rumor mill is. Insufficient information creates the need for more information. The lack of control and abundance of confusion that a nebulous environment brings forces an instinctual quest for information. Curiosity is at the center of why rumors start, and insufficient information feeds rumors. Open communication and dialogue minimize the need for people to fill in the blanks because everyone will be "in-the-know." Companies can control their own rumor mills with greater transparency.

Confidential information is not limited to business information. It also includes personal information. Your ability to hold personal information as sacred speaks about your character. Therefore, it is important that you show restraint when you are entrusted with a secret. Nothing builds trust and confidence like your ability to be discreet, while divulging information haphazardly could label you as weak, gossipy, and untrustworthy. Keeping secrets is not an easy task. The conscious mind struggles not to tell, while impulses of the unconscious want to let the secret slip out. Under pressure, the unconscious mind goes into overdrive and overpowers the conscious mind.

We've all had this happen to us. It is even said that gossiping releases endorphins, just like sex does. Well maybe not **just** like sex, but gossiping does make us feel happy. You know the feeling when you are so immersed in juicy conversation that you actually feel high? It lowers your guard and your sense of vulnerability, which lubricates the lips, making it easy for information to slip out. And when it does, you are riddled with guilt and regret. Maybe it is just like sex after all.

So why do we do it? Why do we feel so compelled to tell a secret when we know that it can be damaging and hurtful to both the victim and to our own credibility? Well, the sheer thrill of knowing something gives us a sense of power and control. It can make us feel important. After all, we know things that others don't. But we don't get that feeling of power unless others know that we know; so somehow, we let them know that we know. It really comes down to ego.

Discretion doesn't only pertain to gossiping about others. It also includes an ability to keep our own secrets. When something consequential occurs in our lives, we all want to share it with someone. I would advise against oversharing at work, especially if the information is highly personal. But people love to talk about themselves. It doesn't take much to get them to reveal their secrets. My brother used to tell me, if you tell just one person your secret then you have told one too many. It's best to keep personal information about yourself in the vault, right next to all the other secrets that you know.

The network of information flows through the path of least resistance. I knew a girl who was having an affair with a Managing Director from another company. She told her work bestie. Her bestie then went out with a former colleague and told her. The former colleague didn't even work in the industry anymore and had even moved out of New York City. But while visiting, she ran into her former supervisor at Starbucks. Excited to see one another, they sat down, had coffee, and caught up on old times. They somehow got to talking, and the girl mentioned that her best friend was having an affair with the MD from another firm. The supervisor was my friend, and she told me. The Managing Director happened to be my boss. Hand to God, this is a true story. Luckily for him, I could keep a secret.

Personal information like this can be extremely inflammatory. I believe this kind of personal information is just that: personal. In a world where privacy is scarce and information is a valued commodity, sharing too much information is bad practice. Even information you think is harmless could be the missing puzzle piece to a much bigger secret. I can't even count how many times I have casually run into someone to later discover that they had been lying about their whereabouts. Busted! But experience has taught me the value of discretion. I try to defend confidentiality at all costs, even if the person is up to no good because it's none of my business and it's none of yours either. *So, mind your own business.* But also keep in mind that if you walk a straight line, then you will have nothing to worry about.

Finally, there is the matter of proper decorum, and we should always be mindful of our surroundings. I got into the elevator early one Friday morning and three other employees followed me in with their breakfasts in hand. They were all quite young, probably in their mid to late twenties. Two were male, and one was female. They began talking amongst themselves, but in a normal conversational volume, so I could easily hear what they were saying. They began by stating how hungover they all were from the night before. Ok, so already an inappropriate work conversation. They began to recap their evening when one of the guys mentioned the girls that randomly strolled into the bar and joined their office gathering. The other guy then said, "I didn't mind because those babes were SMOKING HOT!" I was shocked on many levels, but mostly I was surprised by his stupidity. I turned my head and glared right at him. He paused and then looked at me. My ice-cold stare should have been enough, but just to drive the message home, I said sternly, "Yes, you did say that out loud in a company elevator. And yes, I did hear you." He hung his head low and apologized. Then, he slithered out of the elevator like the snake that he was.

Information comes in many different forms and from various sources. Although it's a valuable commodity, without discretion its value diminishes. In this day and age with technology stripping us of our privacy and exposing our deepest secrets, greater value is placed on confidentiality. In business and in life your ability to keep a secret is worth its weight in gold and the danger of reckless divulgence can be damaging beyond what you might have imagined. Beware of unguarded talk, because loose lips do indeed sink ships.[11]

---

[11] **Loose lips sink ships** is an American English idiom that warns of spilling secrets. The phrase originated on propaganda posters during World War II and was created by the War Advertising Council.

# IT'S ONLY FUNNY 'TIL SOMEONE GETS HURT

**I LOVE TO LAUGH,** but we seem to have lost our sense of humor in this day of political correctness. The intentions of jokes have become misunderstood; instead of being thought of as lighthearted and amusing, they are perceived to be mean-spirited displays of social intolerance. People seem to think that any jab at our differences, always comes from a place of ill intent and someone always seems to feel hurt or offended. In the office what starts out as an attempt to share a laugh, can very quickly go awry, causing damage to the comedian's career. With all the recent discrimination lawsuits, corporations are highly sensitive to issues around diversity and what may begin as something innocent could end up costing the company millions. Therefore, companies take complaints about inappropriate jokes very seriously.

How do you know when you've gone too far? Well, let's first lay out the obvious. Any jokes whatsoever about religion, gender, race, sex or sexual orientation are totally inappropriate for the office. It isn't even a gray area; you just can't do it. Even expressions of slang relating to any of these topics are not acceptable and could potentially escalate to become an

Employee Relations issue. Just last week alone, in two separate conversations, I was affronted to hear comments by two senior employees referring to something as gay like, "that's so gay." I first wondered when this expression made its way back into daily parlance because I haven't heard anyone use it in decades. I then wondered how long before this makes its way to ER because it is one the most prevalent homophobic slurs out there and if it's made a comeback into people's vernaculars, we are going to have some serious issues.

Most office jokes begin rather harmlessly, but inevitably someone takes it too far. This just happened to my young cousin. He called me up in total distress to seek my advice. His story played out exactly as they all do. It began with a bonding moment between his co-workers, telling a few jokes and sharing a few laughs. The jokes were self-deprecating, making fun of themselves and the stereotypes about their own backgrounds and upbringings. Then, one tried to outdo the other. He made a false move and crossed the line, by cutting into someone else's nationality. He just took it a little too far. His mouth opened and the words poured out faster than he could stop them. He wished like hell that he could pull them back in, but he couldn't. He hoped that no one had noticed, but of course, they had. Then, of course, someone took offense, and before he knew it, he received the dreaded phone call from HR. Ugh. I've been there myself. Double ugh, I've been there while I even worked in HR; *you'd think I would have known better.*

Jokes in person can be more easily forgiven than jokes that are written. If you send an inappropriate joke via email, you are pretty much toast. Once you have it in writing, it is out there forever. The most common have been the mistaken "reply to all" or the accidental use of a global distribution list to foolishly share the joy of an obscene joke. The rule of thumb is to never send an email that would embarrass you or your firm if it were printed in the Wall Street Journal. That expression is so widely overused, and yet somehow, people still just can't help themselves and circulate inappropriate quips. If you receive an email with inappropriate content or any profanity, you should delete it immediately. If you forward it on, most company policies consider it to be the same as if you were the originator. And oh, yeah, please be aware that any profanity in email is usually a violation of most Wall Street firm's company policies. It's important to highlight this because, in a recent conversation with my assistant, she said that she was totally unaware of this and swears in e-mail all the time. We also have systems in place that actually screen for profanity, including on mobile devices. If you download company software, such as e-mail, onto your personal device, then in the event of an investigation the firm has the right to examine all of your phone contents, including your personal stuff. So, you'd better think twice before sexting if you are using your personal device to conduct any company business.

The consequences of your actions will depend upon the culture of the firm because a firm's culture dictates what acceptable behavior is. As you know, my formative career years were spent at JP Morgan, which was buttoned-up-tight. So, when I went to Merrill, I suffered from culture shock and was taken back by rather loose behavior. But it wasn't the behavior of the troops that surprised me; it was the behavior of management. I remember when I met the head of one of our sales departments for the second time. He said, "Nice to meet you." I told him that we already had met. He told me he didn't remember me, and that I should consider wearing red stilettos next time because then he definitely would have remembered me. Was this an inappropriate comment? Yes, of course it was. So what did I do about it? I actually let it go. I was new to the firm and didn't want to make waves. Was I offended? It doesn't actually matter. Others were around and heard it. As managers, we both set a poor example; his comments and my inaction set a tone of tolerance and acceptance for this type of behavior. I knew that I had f'd-up on that one.

Then, I began to develop a rapport with this manager. He turned out to be a great guy who was revered by everyone. He was like the mayor, always shaking hands and kissing babies. He was an older gentleman and he was definitely "old school." But that was no excuse. One day, I was wearing a pretty dress as I walked onto the trading floor. I ran into this gent and he said to me "WOW, YOU LOOK FANTASTIC!!" His eyes lit up and he seemed to salivate like a wolf glaring at sheep before pouncing. His remarks continued with exuberance "LET ME CHECK YOU OUT, TURN AROUND!" Well, that comment warranted a call from HR. At the time, I happened to be HR, so I called his boss and told him that we needed to have a chat with this man. His boss asked me if I wanted him to have the conversation. My response was "No" because from what I'd seen of the culture so far, I had no confidence that he'd even know how to deliver the right message. I told him that I would do it myself and I told him exactly the reason. He seemed a bit annoyed by the whole discussion, as if I were a parent that was about to spoil a teenage party. His response to me was "Whatever you need to do, cupcake." Well, that comment, along with his snarky tone was all that was needed to fire me up and I spent most of my days fighting with Merrill's management on their inappropriate behavior.

Inappropriate jokes aren't necessarily limited to the topics I mentioned earlier. They can also just display a lack of overall sensitivity and poor timing. When Merrill, on the verge of collapse, was already bought out by BoA, tensions remained high, as people held onto their jobs for dear life. Most of the management had already been fired, but a few had survived for the purpose of continuity, as the new leadership transitioned in. We knew that bonuses were going to be shit and people were pretty pissed off. As such the rank and file harbored animosity towards any legacy manager that might have had a hand in destroying the beloved ninety-four-year-old firm. One day the legacy divisional head made a comment, which further dented his already suffering popularity. In an attempt at levity, he said to the mortgage traders (the group whose product was responsible for the financial crisis), "Perhaps your wives could hold a bake sale in order to raise money for your bonus pool." Oof. Before you knew it everyone was talking about it. He regretted that comment for the rest of his career. Even now that nearly a decade has passed, he still cringes whenever his kids have a bake sale at school.

All and all, it is important to be aware of your company policies on this topic because cases of inappropriate humor can result in disciplinary actions as severe as termination. I don't want to scare you and I'm sorry to take a topic as light as humor and make it into something heavy. In order to infuse some mirth, I will end this chapter with a joke. Hopefully, you will find it to be amusing and not offensive.

A successful trader parked his brand new Porsche in front of his office ready to show it off to his colleagues. As he got out, a garbage truck sideswiped him and completely tore off the driver's side. The trader immediately grabbed his mobile and dialed 911. Less than 5 minutes later a policeman pulled up, but before he had a chance to ask any questions the trader started screaming about his car. After the trader finished his rant the policemen shook his head in disbelief. "I can't believe how materialistic you traders are," He said, "You're so focused on your possessions you don't notice anything else." "How could you say that?" asked the trader. The policeman replied, "Didn't you realize that your left arm is missing from your elbow down? It's been torn off from when the truck hit you." The trader looked down in absolute horror "Fucking Hell!" he screamed, "Where's my Rolex?!"

# THE PRICE OF LOVE

**I CANNOT WRITE A** book about professionalism without addressing the steamy topic of office romances and affairs in the workplace. Office romances are fairly common; one in four workers gets romantically involved with a colleague at some point during their careers. This isn't surprising; when you spend so much time with a person in such close proximity, it's only natural to develop feelings for them. But office romances are tricky. While nothing has you looking forward to coming to work like a little romance, when it's over, nothing will have you dreading your job more than seeing the ex. Getting over an office breakup is particularly difficult because there is virtually nowhere to hide. Usually, when a relationship ends, "the end" means not seeing one another, but in an office romance, you continue to see each other every single day unless one of you leaves the company.

Most companies have fairly strict policies regarding romantic relationships in the workplace, particularly about relationships in the same department or within the same chain of command – so if you are dating your boss or your boss's boss (or your subordinate for that matter), there is probably a formal policy against it. Companies tend to frown upon office romances because they can be unconstructive distractions affecting productivity and judgment. The very nature of office romances creates a conflict of interest that could lead to bias or favoritism, which can be damaging to the morale of the department.

But just because there are challenges with office relationships, I don't necessarily advise not having them. If you happen to develop feelings for a co-worker and the feelings are reciprocal, then, by all means, go for it. After all, meeting the right person is tough enough, so if you find someone you like, you shouldn't have to pass up the opportunity to date them just because you work together, especially since the long-term success rate of workplace romances is actually quite high. Instead, you should recognize the challenges and learn to manage those challenges carefully. I would also recommend finding out what the company policy is. If it's necessary to disclose the relationship to HR, you may want to consider it, especially if things start getting serious. If you work in the same department, one of you may be asked to transfer. Be mindful of your interactions, and be sensitive to the people around you. Try to behave in a professional manner, while keeping the relationship as low key as possible. I won't go so far as to tell you to keep your relationship a secret because you likely won't be able to. And if you think that people aren't going to find out, then you are being naïve.

The same holds true for an office affair. If you think you can successfully conceal an office affair from your co-workers, then you are kidding yourself. You actually have a better chance of keeping a legitimate relationship secret, because affairs tend to pique more interest and attract more attention. The reason they know is that affairs don't just suddenly happen. They tend to develop over time. All of the non-verbal cues between you and your lover have been observed by your co-workers all along.

Often, your flirtatious body language gives you away, even before the affair goes full throttle. Then, when you overlay patterns of behavior, such as simultaneous time away from the office, it becomes obvious. And that's all that's needed for the rumor to go viral around the office. Then there is the inevitable accidental encounter with a co-worker who just happens to run into you and your lover in a place where neither of you should be together. That's the slam-dunk that confirms the rumor. No matter how clever you think you are, or how careful and discreet you think you have been, everyone probably already knows about your affair.

My advice about office affairs is not to have them because they almost always end badly. Putting morality aside for a moment, when getting into a relationship where one or both people are already committed, someone is going to get hurt. And that someone is usually the woman because women tend to come out of affairs more battered than men. Men, on the whole, are better at compartmentalizing their lives between spouse and lover. They are also better at coping with compromising their morals. Most importantly, they are better at keeping their jobs when the affair becomes public. Affairs in the workplace never end well, and when they end, they tend to be very destructive, causing damage to more than just the infidels.

Men tend to recover from an office affair much better than women, as people are more forgiving of men who cheat than women who cheat. Even today, women are labeled with a scarlet letter, and nothing damages a woman's reputation like an office affair. When a woman has an office affair, it follows her pretty much for the rest of her career; she might as well put it on her resume under Interests and Hobbies, right after Reading.

In addition to damaging your reputation, an office affair can result in the loss of your job and the destruction of your marriage. Yet, the workplace is the number one place for married people to engage in infidelity (85% of all affairs begin in the office). With so much to lose, it seems rather surprising that so many would take the risk. But trying to talk someone out of having an affair is usually a futile exercise. After all, the heart wants what the heart wants (which is just so cliché). In fact, the whole notion of an office affair is rather cliché. But regardless, affairs continue to occur. As a word of warning, if you happen to find yourself in a situation where an attraction sparks between you and your married co-worker, and he or she begins feeding you the lines that typically precede an affair, I suggest that you turn around and walk away. Actually don't walk, run, run before it's too late. If you're not sure what those lines sound like, here is just a small sample:

- My wife doesn't understand me [like you do]
- My needs at home aren't being met
- I We deserve this

Why are office affairs so tantalizing? Well, an affair creates an illusion of love, while feelings of intoxication fuel the fantasy. Because affairs are isolated from reality, they are free from the mundane activities of daily life, which is part of their appeal. The absence of reality helps bolster the passion, while the risk of being caught raises the intensity and adds to the excitement. Late nights at the office and business travel with expense accounts foster opportunity.

It's almost too hard to resist when the temptation is so near. But if you find yourself contemplating an affair, you may want to step back for a moment and think about what might be missing in your life that has made you so vulnerable to infidelity. Often, an affair is a symptom of greater unhappiness, which might be worth exploring <u>before</u> you veer down a path where the damage could be irreversible. If you are single, you should try to understand why you're putting yourself into a situation that will ultimately result in pain. Because honey, the truth of the matter is that at the end of the day, men don't leave their wives for mistresses. Ok, some do, but it's extremely rare. And when they do, the chances that your relationship will survive the divorce are slim.

# BRAND-AID

**IN THE COMPETITIVE ENVIRONMENT** of the business world, what differentiates you from others is your brand. The value of your brand is determined by the credibility that you've established through consistent behaviors over time. When properly managed, your brand is an asset, which can open doors of opportunity and pave the way to a successful career. But as I've demonstrated by my own mistakes, a poor brand, even if created by unintentional mistakes, may have the opposite effect; it could shut you out of opportunities and hurt your career. But repairing your brand once it is damaged is entirely possible. As you've seen in my situation, I was able to recover from the wreckage and went on to have a vibrant and prosperous career.

The strongest personal brands are based on authentic values, reflected in your passions and strengths, and reinforced by your behaviors. A disconnect between your values and your behaviors will most certainly have an impact on your brand. For example, if loyalty is one of your core values, yet you frequently maneuver in a way that hurts your colleagues, you will become known as untrustworthy and conniving. This will have a negative effect on your brand. Often times, our core values are good, but the environment we're in brings out the worst in us. A bad culture can reinforce poor behaviors. This is especially true in highly competitive and cutthroat environments. It is, therefore, necessary to check yourself regularly and make sure that your behaviors are in lock step with your values. As always, awareness is an instrumental part of this exercise and, as such, it is the common denominator of pretty much every topic discussed in this book.

When you are striving for career advancement, a continual investment in your brand is a wise step. You always want your brand to project the best version of yourself. Having a clear goal about how you want people to feel about you is a necessary part of that. You will also want to develop a brand strategy, which consists of certain actions and behaviors that will help form an impression of you. I suggest making a list. This list should also include any hidden qualities that you want to bring to the forefront, even if they are out of your comfort zone. No one said this was going to be easy. Creating the right brand can be a challenging assignment for some, so you should expect it to be uncomfortable at first. When making your list, try to also identify your blind spots, which are any negative perceptions you are already creating with your behaviors. If you aren't sure, then you should ask someone to tell you the honest truth. But the truth might sting a little, so brace yourself. And once you've asked for feedback, you can't become defensive or angry. Instead, you should thank the person for their honesty and show them your sincere gratitude. Asking close personal friends and family isn't always the best way to develop your professional identity, because your behavior at the office may be different than your behaviors in your personal life. Ask a close colleague or a mentor instead.

Even after you've carefully created your brand, it is not

uncommon to have missteps. When you do, don't beat yourself up about it or wallow in despair. Instead, take the necessary measures to fix the issue. The first step in brand repair is to assess the damage. Evaluate the impact of your actions in order to get a sense of what the cost will be to your career. Through a realistic lens, calculate the level of control that you actually have over the situation and whether or not you can mend this yourself. You may need to solicit additional help from a boss, mentor, or even a coach. When asking for help, be sure to go to someone you trust who has your best interest at heart. Then, develop a plan for brand repair. Keep in mind that brand repair works through consistent repetition and takes discipline and commitment. You will also need time and patience.

Here is a simple case of brand repair.

- Perception/Brand: Unreliable and Disorganized
- Impressions:
  - Disheveled appearance
  - Always seems stressed or out of control
- Actions that contribute to perceptions:
  - Frequently late for work
  - Chronic absenteeism
  - Tardy for meetings
  - Not showing up to meetings
  - Messy workspace
- Assess your work performance:
  - Failure to meet some deadlines
  - Unresponsive to e-mails and phone calls

Brand Repair: Implore new good habits
that create an improved brand

- Re-adjust your work schedule to arrive 30 minutes earlier than usual; this includes having your coffee and breakfast in hand.

Use this extra time to get organized.

- Take time in the morning to review the schedule of the day ahead. Know where you need to be and when.
- Use the extra time to listen to voicemails and check e-mails that you've received overnight. Identify the ones that are most critical and require immediate attention. Quickly skim through the rest until you have time to go back and thoroughly read them.
- Tidy your desk each day before you leave work.
- Work late one night a week to clean up your desk and get yourself organized.
- Figure out how to complete your projects on time. Work smarter, not necessarily harder.
- Pay closer attention to your overall appearance, including your fashion choices and your body language.
- Read: *Getting Things Done* by: David Allen

*Brand repair will require your actions to go above and beyond what is typical. Once you have fixed your brand, you can normalize your actions and behaviors.

The strategy outlined above is relatively straightforward because it is based on tangible action items. But sometimes our issues are much more complex and require greater introspection into your identity. For example, what should you do when the prickly style of your temperament causes you to become universally disliked? A severe character flaw may require a complete brand overhaul, which could be difficult to achieve on your own. For this, I recommend using a career coach, because you will also need someone to help you re-write the narrative of your brand recovery strategy.

I myself used a coach at different points in my career. One coach, in particular, was hired by my company to help soften my aggressive personality, which was off-putting to my colleagues. We worked tirelessly, but still, we struggled to find the right hook on which I could hang my new image. I think my coach was just about ready to give up when she suggested that we leave the office and go out to lunch. Taking me out of the work environment and mixing up the venue made me feel comfortable enough to get personal. I let my guard down and began to show a more vulnerable side. My coach was floored. She seemed surprised to hear about my struggles and hardships and began to feel compassion. She learned about my interests and passions and heard about what inspired me. For the first time, I think she actually started to like me. Nevertheless, we seemed to have found the breakthrough that we were looking for.

My coach urged me to exhibit more of my appealing and empathetic qualities to aid in my brand repair. As part of my re-branding effort, she encouraged me to reveal more about my personal life at work. I followed her instruction and even made it my own. So I did what most career coaches would advise you

NOT to do. I baked cookies for the office. Baking has been a passion of mine since my seventh birthday when I received my first Betty Crocker Easy Bake Oven. So that holiday season, I baked up some of my famous sweet treats and packaged them up in pretty holiday wrapping, perfectly tied with Christmas bows, and left them on peoples' desks with little note cards attached. I was a regular Martha fuckin' Stewart.

As my re-branding work continued, I selectively and carefully shared stories about my personal life. I provided the details that were appealing to my audience and I omitted those parts that were less palatable. As an example, I talked about learning how to make Chicken Tagine in Morocco, but I skipped the details about how I actually killed the chicken with my own bare hands. Details like that weren't necessarily conducive to creating my softer image. It took a few months, but the transformation did start to take hold, and my colleagues responded positively. The re-brand was working. I finally understood what I needed to do and how I needed to behave - I really just needed to be more human.

I stopped treating people like they were tools that I used to get my job done. I looked back to my days at Acme when I was moved by people's personal stories and remembered how much they inspired me and even enriched my life. Yet, somehow along the way in my intense quest for success, I lost sight of what was important and I stopped valuing human connections. I knew that I needed to get back to that, not just for the sake of my career, but for me and for the sake of my soul.

So I took the time to get to know my colleagues on a personal level and alas, friendships started to form. One night, several months later we all went out to dinner and the topic of the Christmas cookies came up. My colleagues told me that when they received them, they couldn't figure out who they were from, despite the writing on the card stating that they were from me. In disbelief and confusion, they all called one another to see if anyone knew who delivered these mysterious treats. There was only one Tamara in the entire firm, yet they wouldn't accept that the cookies were from me. When they finally gave into the possibility, they paused for a moment and began to wonder if the cookies might have been poisoned. We laughed about it that night but WOW was it a harsh realization of what an awful person my brand portrayed. Enough said.

# SOME CLOSING THOUGHTS TO MY DEAR MILLENNIALS

**FOR AS LONG AS** I can remember, I've wanted to work on Wall Street. After relentless perseverance, I achieved this goal and found my place in an industry that inspired my ambitions. But the industry was far from perfect, as gender discrimination seemed to be woven into the fabric of its culture. Although there are many examples of women achieving great success in financial services, the industry hasn't done enough to create an environment where diversity flourishes. Women who have reached the annals of the C-Suite are much more of an anomaly than they are the norm. Throughout my career, I have done what I could to help women navigate this industry. But as I take stock in the impact of my actions, I realize that while I may have had an effect on a few individuals, my overall impact didn't move the needle in any meaningful way. I now recognize that collective action is required in order to make a difference for the greater good. But I am as hopeful and inspired as ever. And here is why?

The Millennials have begun to join the workforce, and your impact will be seismic. That's right, you heard me correctly.

Your generation, which has been labeled "entitled," has the potential to have the greatest influence on workforce culture that we have ever seen. And it is this very characteristic of "entitled" that gives you the confidence needed to challenge the status quo because, in your hearts, you believe that you deserve it. And you do. In fact, we all do. So, with the collective actions of your civic-minded generation, we have the opportunity to change corporate culture for the better.

When it comes to your careers, you tend to bring your values into the workplace. You are willing to fight for what you believe and much of what you believe in is based on fairness. I view this as our greatest chance to make a real difference. I am hopeful that you can help reshape the workplace, to make diversity and equitability a part of its foundation and not merely quotas to which companies adhere.

The impact of your generation is no surprise to anyone on Wall Street as we planned for your arrival all along. Circa 2004, corporate management geared up for Gen Y to join the workforce by hiring loads of consultants to help train us and retool us with new management principles. We were told that your generation would redefine all the rules because you weren't going to fall in line as previous generations had done. We were therefore expected to change our methods in order to adapt to you. We were warned that your generation would polarize production if our arcane management styles didn't shift to become softer and more embracing.

Although we prepared for this, it seemed to have snuck up on us anyway. In 2005, Gen Y joined the workforce and just like Y2K, your cataclysmic impact didn't materialize right away. Instead, your entrance into the workforce was overshadowed by another cataclysmic event, the financial crisis of 2008. As the world economy imploded, no one really paid any attention to you. With the backdrop of economic upheaval and a contracting job market, your entrance into the workforce was much more subtle than originally expected. But as the economy continued to improve over the years, more Millennials joined the workforce and now the impact of your presence is finally being felt.

But your revolutionary spirit needs to be properly harnessed otherwise another generation will pass us by, making little progress. And enthusiasm alone is not enough. Systemic change takes time and perseverance. Whether or not you have the longevity and the fortitude to fight for the long haul is yet to be determined. And although we have seen your generation stand up for what you believe, we have also seen you walk out the door when you are dissatisfied. And while these actions have caught the attention of the management, your generation will need to provide solutions in order to help us change the system from within. It is also important to build on the knowledge and wisdom of previous generations and to recognize the value of experience. We can all learn from each other, by replicating your collaborative nature and working together for the greater good.

Many companies are already shifting their management practices to align with the principles of your generation. Many of you are even managers yourselves with an ability to influence within your own organizations. Everywhere I look, more mindful management styles are emerging and companies are putting social responsibility at the forefront of their business models. These are all positive and noble changes for which we can thank your generation, as you have helped set the course for this new direction. And if anyone thinks that this is merely a trend, then they are wrong. The momentum will only continue as more Millennials join the workforce.

But is your generation really all that different from my generation? Probably not, because we were all idealistic when we were young. But one major difference is that you seem to be unwilling to settle in order to conform to an idea or a system in which you don't believe. You tend to voice your dissatisfaction and will stand by your convictions with your actions. That is a major difference between your generation and the previous generations of Gen X and even the Baby Boomers. I grew up as part of a generation that was told that the world doesn't really give a shit about what you think. We were taught that the way to succeed in life was to fall in line and to follow the rules. So we did, just as the previous generation before us, had done. As a result, we haven't seen dramatic social change in over a generation. Furthermore, my generation is probably the most dissatisfied when it comes to career choices and finding our true purpose. It took me years, even decades to discover my own self-worth and to understand that we all have special gifts to offer the world. But you seem to understand this right out of the gate. And although older generations may poo-poo you for what they deplore as self-absorbed qualities, I applaud you for having enough self-respect to demand better. It is this type of mindset that has limitless potential. It is this type of mindset that will change the world. SO, GO GET 'EM!

Printed in the United States
By Bookmasters